Katherine

T0285739

111 Places in Bournemouth That You Shouldn't Miss

Photographs by Oliver Smith

emons:

For Ben, Josh and Toby: my brilliant, Bournemouth boys

© Emons Verlag GmbH
All rights reserved
© Photographs by Oliver Smith, except:
Jan Tupper – Arniss Equestrian (ch. 8); Conker (ch. 29); Jamie James – GIANT
Gallery (ch. 50); La Fosse (ch. 58); Mark Eaton – Silent Yoga UK (ch. 89)
© Cover icon: shutterstock.com/Martin Parratt
Layout: Editorial Design & Artdirection, Conny Laue,
based on a design by Lübbeke | Naumann | Thoben
Maps: altancicek.design, www.altancicek.de
Basic cartographical information from Openstreetmap,
© OpenStreetMap-Mitwirkende, OdbL
Editing: Ros Horton
Printing and binding: Grafisches Centrum Cuno, Calbe
Printed in Germany 2022
ISBN 978-3-7408-1166-2
First edition

Did you enjoy this guidebook? Would you like to see more?
Join us in uncovering new places around the world at
www.111places.com

Foreword

Growing up in Bournemouth, I had a wonderful time: playing on the beach, splashing through the River Bourne in my wellies, riding the 'Noddy' train at Hengistbury Head… But, crikey, it's only now that I've written this book do I realise how much I was missing out on! I had no idea, for example, that I could have been visiting an Egyptian mummy, gazing into the real Alice in Wonderland's mirror or making magic in the woods, in memory of a local witch.

During the course of researching and writing this book, I've had breakfast with The Beatles, lunch with 11 feline friends, and drinks with Charlie Chaplin. I tried to share a bottle of wine with Napoléon but, unfortunately, his stash was cleared out. I've slept under the stars on Boscombe Beach, bought a loaf of bread from where the fugitives of the Great Train Robbery were hiding out, and labelled my own bottle of gin – exploring areas such as Christchurch, Mudeford, Kinson, Southbourne and Highcliffe. I haven't journeyed in the direction of Poole because those areas are covered in my other book, *111 Places in Poole That You Shouldn't Miss*. Many of the spots in this guidebook aren't in Bournemouth proper. I've jaunted as far as the New Forest, always keeping within about a 30-minute drive of central Bournemouth. Who doesn't love a day trip?

I have done my absolute best to ensure that my facts are correct, but if you notice any inaccuracies, please accept my apologies (and don't tell anyone else!). As you read this book, my hope is that, like me, you find many new, exciting, surprising places to delve into. Or unearth fun, fascinating facts about places you already know and love. If you venture to Hengistbury Head, you should certainly take a ride on the 'Noddy' train. It really never gets old.

111 Places

1 Adventure Wonderland Maze

Hedge your bets

Left? Right? This way? That way? Argh, another dead end! Just like Alice (see ch. 6), you may find yourself lost in this maze – one of the largest in the UK. Covering 1.25 acres of Adventure Wonderland theme park, and consisting of 1.7 miles of paths and 5,200 bushes, this octagonal beech hedge maze was designed in 1991 by Bournemouth-born Adrian Fisher, now the world's greatest maze maker.

Enter this loopy labyrinth and you'll navigate many *Alice in Wonderland* characters. With a bird's eye view, from the top, clockwise, there's Alice, Mad Hatter, White Rabbit, Cheshire Cat, Queen of Hearts, Gryphon, Mock Turtle and Dodo. The centre portrays the White Rabbit's pocket watch, with steps up and down the mound indicating four o'clock, perpetual teatime in middle-class England. The central octagon is a giant teapot, with the Dormouse asleep in the handle.

Having built his first maze in his parents' garden at Throop House in Bournemouth in 1975, Adrian has gone on to design more than 700 mazes in 42 countries. He uses hedges, wooden panels, water, paving, maize and mirrors (his company is the leading supplier of mirror mazes worldwide). His Throop House maze, however, was constructed from holly, which he now concedes should be avoided 'for obvious reasons'. That said, you don't get any cheating with a holly hedge!

Awarded an MBE in 2020 for services to international trade and creative industries, Adrian holds eight Guinness World Records. Living near Blandford in Dorset, his home has a mind-bending maze, and a tapestry of the Alice maze hangs in his studio. Adrian's meandering creativity knows no bounds, and if you manage to find the Wonderland maze exit, you'll leave in a flurry of playing cards, just as Alice did. After your winding adventure, why not head to The Wild Thing Cafe? You'll certainly have earned yourself a cup of tea.

Address Adventure Wonderland, Merritown Lane, Hurn, Christchurch BH23 6BA, +44 (0)1202 483444, www.adventurewonderland.co.uk and www.mazemaker.com | Getting there Bus 737 to Adventure Wonderland | Hours Check the website as opening hours vary | Tip Head to the theme park's other bushy attraction, the Shrinking Hedge, and try your luck at the interactive *Alice in Wonderland* quiz.

2 AFC Bournemouth Trophies
Back of the net!

How much did AFC Bournemouth's top-earning player reportedly earn each week in the 2020/21 season? A whopping £73,000. Striker Ted MacDougall – who made history by scoring nine goals in one match in 1971 – was paid a weekly wage of £150. In 1912, the club's first professional player, Harry Baven Penton, took home 30 shillings a week. Times – and salaries – have changed. What hasn't changed is the fact that the team has always scored victories.

In 1906, Boscombe Football Club (it became AFC Bournemouth in 1972 to create a slick image, and also so it'd be top of alphabetical club lists) won its first trophy in the Hampshire Junior Cup. Many more followed, including the Russell-Cotes Cup (see ch. 67). For years, the trophies were kept in the boardrooms but, in 2015, when the club got promoted to the Premier League (sadly, they were relegated in 2020), this trophy cabinet was built to display the team's accomplishments. *Up the Cherries!*

During its first two seasons, the team played on a pitch on Castlemain Avenue but, in 1910, moved to the current site, then called Dean Court, named after the landowner James Cooper-Dean. There were no dressing rooms in the early days, so the lads changed at the Portman Hotel, then trudged across Kings Park to the ground, which was next to cherry orchards. It's said this is one of the reasons for the nickname 'the Cherries' – the other being the cherry-red stripes on the kit.

Money was originally too tight for a committee room, so meetings were held and teams selected under street lamps in Pokesdown. The one at 112 Haviland Road holds particular significance, with Boscombe FC being formed under it in 1899. The first 'proper' meeting was at 60 Gladstone Road. If it hadn't been for the passion (and willingness to get rained on under a lamppost) of these footie enthusiasts, AFC Bournemouth may never have existed. They deserve a medal. Or perhaps even a trophy.

Address AFC Bournemouth Superstore, Vitality Stadium, Kings Park, BH7 7AF, +44 (0)3445 761910, www.afcb.co.uk | Getting there Bus 2 to Kings Park | Hours Mon – Fri 9am – 5pm, Sat 9.30am – 4pm, Sun 10am – 3pm. Times vary on match days; see the website for details | Tip In 1902, to mark the occasion of the coronation of King Edward VII and Queen Alexandra of Denmark, Bournemouth Council agreed to rename common No. 59 Kings Park and common No. 60 Queens Park.

3 AIDS Tile Tributes

I want to break free

Freddie Mercury, Rock Hudson, Liberace: these men all famously died as a result of AIDS. Michael, John, Costas: these men also died as a result of AIDS, and have been remembered here, along with around 400 others. Every tile in this memorial was designed by a local schoolchild and represents a person in Dorset to have succumbed to the disease. Unveiled on World Aids Day in 2009, the project was created by Andrew Armstrong, who was diagnosed with HIV in the 1980s, and who set up charity DAMSET (Dorset Aids Memorial Schools Education Trust) in 1999 to educate people about the disease, as there are still misconceptions about it.

Many people believe that, after the 1980s AIDS crisis, HIV/AIDS is now an 'African problem' but, in 2019, around 105,200 people were living with it in the UK, about 900 in the BCP (Bournemouth, Poole and Christchurch) areas. Around a decade ago, Bournemouth had the fourth highest prevalence rate for HIV in the UK outside London, and more than half of the diagnoses in Dorset were of heterosexual, non-injecting drug users. Thankfully, the rate of infection is decreasing every year. The government has committed to ending HIV transmissions in England by 2030.

Up until 2021, the first man to have died from AIDS in the UK was believed to be Terrence Higgins, but an ITV investigation revealed it to actually be John Eaddie, who ran a guesthouse in Bournemouth, and died in 1981.

In June, 2021, the Dine & Disco annual event was held at Chewton Glen (see ch. 26), where Rick Astley, former Spice Girl Melanie C and Sir Elton John performed, helping to raise more than £1.9 million for the Elton John AIDS Foundation. David Furnish, Elton's husband, unveiled a bronze AIDS memorial in Brighton in 2009, which – along with the Bournemouth AIDS memorial – is one of only a handful of artworks in the world dedicated to victims of HIV and AIDS.

Address Pier Approach, BH2 5AA | Getting there An 8-minute walk from Bournemouth Square, through the Lower Gardens. The memorial is in the underpass between the gardens and Pier Approach. | Tip Bournemouth-based artist David A. Lindon (www.davidalindon.com) made headlines with his microscopic art that fits inside the eye of a needle, some pieces commanding as much as £15,000. One of his mini masterpieces? Freddie Mercury.

4 Airfields Memorial
We have lift-off

Captain Darrell R. Lindsey of the US Army Air Force was a brave man. He stayed at the controls of his burning B-26 Marauder bomber aircraft on 9 August, 1944 to allow his crew to escape. In doing so, he lost his life and was awarded a Medal of Honor posthumously. It was from near this site – the former Holmsley South Airfield – that his mission was led, and where the New Forest Airfields Memorial has stood since 2002.

This monument, with a Dakota aircraft propeller as a focal point (and a time capsule within, due to be unearthed in 2045), honours Captain Lindsey, and the people who worked at the New Forest's 12 airfields between 1939 and 1945. During the D-Day period in June 1944, 25,000 military personnel, supported by 10,000 civilians, were deployed on the airfields. One of the military men was Barack Obama's grandpa, who worked at Stoney Cross as an armourer.

The 12 airfields – Holmsley South, Stoney Cross, Beaulieu, Hurn, Ibsley, Calshot, Christchurch, Sway, Needs Oar Point, Lymington, Winkton and Bisterne – played a vital role in the victory of World War II, and in bringing home thousands of prisoners of war. Around D-Day, hundreds of missions were flown; Needs Oar Point was the busiest airfield in the country for three weeks, with takeoffs and landings every 45 seconds. Evidence of the airfields can still be seen. At Beaulieu Heath, sections of the runways and perimeter road remain, as does the 10-foot-high Pundit Code 'BL', which would have identified the base from the air.

To learn more, head to the FONFA (Friends of the New Forest Airfields) Heritage Centre, where you'll find model aircraft, war artefacts, photos, uniforms, pilots' stories, and prints of the aircraft, most of which are signed by the pilots and ground crew. Commemorative services are held at the memorial on Armed Forces Day, Remembrance Day and US Memorial Day. Lest we forget.

1939 - 1945
NEW FOREST AIRFIELDS

BEAULIEU | HURN | CHRIST CHURCH | CALSHOT | STONEY CROSS

WINKTON | NEEDS OAR POINT | BISTERNE | SWAY | IBSLEY | LYMINGTON | HOLMSLEY SOUTH

Address Black Lane, Holmsley South, Bransgore, Christchurch BH23 8EB, www.fonfasite. wordpress.com | Getting there By car, brown signs indicate the way from the A35 Lyndhurst to Christchurch road. About 3.5 miles from Hinton Admiral train station | Tip To pay your respects to more brave souls who served in World War II, head to the Canadian War Memorial in Lyndhurst, SO43 7GQ. In the run-up to D-Day, it was at this site that Canadians of all denominations stationed in the New Forest would meet for services with the local chaplain.

5 The Alice Lisle

She lost her head

If you Google 'people who have been beheaded', you'll be met with an alarmingly long Wikipedia list – with most victims having hailed from England. Two of Henry VIII's wives – Anne Boleyn and Catherine Howard – are on the list and, if you keep scrolling, you'll see Lady Alice Lisle's name. On 2 September, 1685, Alice was the last woman in England to be beheaded, and this New Forest pub is named after her.

The 67-year-old widow's crime? She harboured two fugitives – John Hickes and Richard Nelthorpe – after the Battle of Sedgemoor, at her home, Moyles Court (now Moyles Court School), less than half a mile from here. John was found by officials in the malthouse, while Richard was discovered in the chimney. Despite the jury finding Alice not guilty three times, the ruthless Judge Jeffreys intimidated them so much that they changed the verdict to guilty. The poor woman's fate was sealed as soon as the infamous 'Hanging Judge' took the case (if you thought Judge Judy was harsh…). Originally sentenced to being burned at the stake, this was later changed to beheading.

Alice's mother was Edith Bond, a relative of spy John Bond, who is said to have inspired Ian Fleming's 007 character. Inside The Alice Lisle pub, you can learn more about the condemned woman, and see pictures relating to the case, including one of her being arrested. If you'd rather not learn about the gruesome tale before tucking into your fish and triple-cooked chips, sit in the 450-capacity beer garden and take in the view of Rockford Lake.

Back inside, there are photos of schoolchildren, complete with cheeky smiles and grazed knees. They were pupils of Rockford Primary School, which is what the building was until 1941. You'll also see framed books, such as *The Ladybird Book of Handwriting*, and a statement wall of fountain-pen wallpaper. As was the case for Alice, the writing is on the wall.

Address Rockford Green, Rockford, Ringwood BH24 3NA, +44 (0)1425 474700, www.thealicelisle.co.uk | Getting there Bus X3 to Ellingham Crossroads, then a 20-minute walk | Hours Mon–Thu 11am–10pm, Fri & Sat 11am–10.30pm, Sun noon–9.30pm | Tip The Ibsley Room inside the pub is dedicated to Ibsley Airfield, about a mile away, where a memorial now stands (different from the one in ch. 4). Filming took place here for the 1942 movie *The First of the Few*, in which you can see many of the buildings at Ibsley, including the control tower and hangars.

6   Alice's Mirror
We're all mad here

Mirror, mirror, on the wall... No, wait, wrong story. This mirror didn't belong to the Evil Queen, but Alice in Wonderland. More accurately, Alice Hargreaves (née Liddell), who inspired Charles Dodgson (pen name, Lewis Carroll) to create his adventures of the inquisitive girl who fell down a rabbit hole. On 4 July, 1862, while rowing down the River Thames in Oxford, Dodgson dreamt up a story to entertain 10-year-old Alice and her two sisters. At Alice's insistence, he wrote the tale down, and it became the manuscript *Alice's Adventures Under Ground* (published in 1865 as *Alice's Adventures in Wonderland*), which he gifted to Alice.

After marrying Reginald Hargreaves in 1880, Alice moved to Cuffnells mansion in Lyndhurst, which is where this gilt-framed 'looking glass' was hung. The *Alice's Adventures Under Ground* manuscript was also kept here, accessible for visitors to leaf through. In 1928, facing financial hardship, Alice was forced to sell the text, which fetched £15,400 at auction, nearly four times the reserve price.

Note the two fake red and white rose bushes standing next to the mirror, and spare a thought for the poor Card Soldiers, who were caught during their flower-painting mission by the murderous Queen of Hearts: 'Off with their heads!'. Then turn your attention to the 25-foot-long New Forest Embroidery and challenge yourself to a game of 'Where's Alice?'.

Just up the road, at the Church of St Michael and All Angels, Alice's ashes are buried, alongside real red and white rose bushes. Alice was an active parishioner of this church, with her sons – Alan, Leopold and Caryl – being christened here. Alan and Leopold died in World War I, and their names can be found on the memorial at Bolton's Bench (see ch. 17), which their mother helped to design. Many believed that Caryl was named after 'Lewis Carroll', but Alice denied this to be true. Curiouser and curiouser...

Address New Forest Heritage Centre, Lyndhurst, Hampshire SO43 7NY, +44 (0)2380 283444, www.newforestheritage.org.uk | Getting there About 4 miles from Brockenhurst train station. The mirror is on the first floor of the museum. | Hours Apr–Oct 10am–5pm, Nov–Mar 10am–4pm | Tip For a little 'eat-me/drink-me' action, head to The Mad Hatter Tea Rooms (www.madhatterlyndhurst.co.uk) very near to the Church of St Michael and All Angels. The Mad Hatter Prosecco High Tea will leave you grinning like the Cheshire Cat.

7 Anne Frank's Tree
Branches of hope

'Think of all the beauty still left around you and be happy.' Sound advice from the teenage diarist hiding in an attic in Amsterdam for more than two years during World War II. Anne Frank is an international icon for hope, after her diary documenting her time in this Secret Annex was published in 1947, then translated into over 70 languages. *The Diary of Anne Frank* is the most widely read non-fiction book in the English language after the Bible. Despite Anne's death at the age of 15 (she was one of the 1.5 million Jewish children killed by the Nazis during the Holocaust), her legacy lives on. This horse chestnut tree was planted on 12 June, 1998, and commemorates Anne and all children killed in wars and conflicts in the 20th century.

The Anne Frank Trust UK was founded in 1990 by Bournemouth local Gillian Walnes Perry (who grew up in San Remo Towers – see ch. 85), Rabbi David Soetendorp, Bee Klug (both living in Bournemouth and friends of Otto Frank, Anne's father) and Holocaust survivor and posthumous stepsister of Anne Frank, Dr Eva Schloss. The only organisation in the UK licensed to use Anne Frank's name and writing to make links with issues in modern society, the charity uses Anne's story as a starting point to empower young people to challenge prejudice. It works with schools, local authorities and criminal justice education services to deliver exhibitions and workshops that reach more than 50,000 young people a year.

Gillian's book, *The Legacy of Anne Frank*, has been described as a 'handbook of hope', and chronicles the impact Anne had on people such as Audrey Hepburn, who became one of The Anne Frank Trust's first patrons in 1991, and Nelson Mandela. There is also a lot about Bournemouth in the book.

As you stand by Anne's tree, look at all the beauty around you – the towering trees, flowing stream, friends heading for a tennis game – and be happy.

Address Bournemouth Central Gardens, Bourne Avenue, BH2 6DJ | **Getting there** Enter the gardens by the Bournemouth War Memorial and head to the other side of the stream. Turn right and walk for about a minute; the tree is before the tennis courts. | **Tip** Stroll around the gardens and you'll find a tree planted in memory of Diana, Princess of Wales, another woman who inspired many. It's an English oak fastigiata and is beside a bench also dedicated to her.

8 Arniss Equestrian
Drifting along

'What do we need that the forest cannot provide? We have food, wood for weapons, we'll find safety and solace in our trees.' This was said by Kevin Costner in the 1991 blockbuster *Robin Hood: Prince of Thieves*, some of which was filmed in the New Forest. On Arniss Equestrian's Discover Tour, you'll be taken on one of their 20 horses through Pitts Wood, where the Celts-battling scene was filmed, plus the scenes with the wooden treehouses. You'll also see the sites of World War II bombing range Ashley Walk (see ch. 11).

As well as providing food, wood and safety for a gutsy outlaw – and target practice for the Royal Air Force – the 140,000-acre forest also provides a home for some 9,000 livestock (cattle, sheep, donkeys, mules and pigs), around 3,000 of which are New Forest ponies. Although disputed, legend has it that horses escaped from sinking ships in the Spanish Armada in 1588, swimming ashore to establish these herds of wild horses. Each of these animals is owned by one of the 500 New Forest 'commoners' – a title that's been around since 1217 and holds more status than it sounds. Commoners have the right to graze their animals here, meaning the New Forest is basically one giant farm.

Every year, during the months of May and June, carefully selected stallions are released to join the mares. Around 11 months later, an influx of cute foals trot into the world. Between August and November, the New Forest Drift takes place, when the commoners round up their horses for health checks and to decide which ones will remain wild, which ones will be taken to fields, and which ones will be sold (Arniss Equestrian own five New Forest horses).

As you're hacking through the forest on your trusty steed, your mind may do some drifting of its own. Taking in the light dancing through the trees, you'll likely think: 'There's nothing I need that the forest cannot provide… at least for the next two hours'.

Address Godshill, Fordingbridge SP6 2JX, +44 (0)1425 654114, www.arnissequestrian.co.uk | Getting there Bus X3 to Fordingbridge Post Office, then a 40-minute walk or 8-minute taxi ride | Hours Times of rides vary, so contact the stables for details | Tip Head to The Cartwheel Inn (www.cartwheelinnwhitsbury.com) for lunch, behind which is Whitsbury Manor Stables, the former home of champion racehorse Desert Orchid.

9 Artcetera
Been there, done that... framed the T-shirt

Paintings, photographs, football shirts, butterflies, rugby balls, fossils, babygros, war medals, keys, car pieces from a Formula 1 crash, toys, boxing gloves, a wooden Tiki man, a speedway suit, a Las Vegas casino chip, 3D maps, Banksy prints, bomb fragments, a metal poppy from the 2014 art exhibition at the Tower of London, a deer skin... You name it, Artcetera has framed it. One of Bournemouth's oldest framing and art supplies shops, it was taken over by Harry and Ivy Jarvis in 1970, when it was a DIY store.

In 1976, the creative couple displayed their first rack of Daler-Rowney Georgian Oil Paint and never looked back. They threw out the plungers and replaced them with paints, paintbrushes, palettes, pencils, pens, pastels, paper, pads, primers, portfolios and pantographs (plus other art materials that don't begin with the letter 'p'). Harry and Ivy's daughter, Caryn, started working at the shop in June 1977 and is still there now.

A member of the Fine Art Trade Guild, which sets exacting standards in the art and framing industry, Artcetera has framed around 100,000 items in its time, now averaging 50 to 60 pieces a week. Customers select from the 400-plus frame options, and then Caryn and the team use five different machines to mitre, underpin, glass-cut, press and mount, to produce the final product. A sign in the shop warns: *Uncollected pictures will be deemed the property of Artcetera if left longer than a period of 12 months.* The framed (of course) notice is dated 'June 1988' but is still enforced today.

One customer who has been using Artcetera's framing service and art supplies since way before 1988 is fantasy artist Josephine Wall, who has a gallery in Penn Hill. Another artist, Igor Moritz, who worked at Artcetera between 2014 and 2019 – and now exhibits his work all over the world – left a parting gift in the form of a self-portrait oil painting, which is hung by the door.

Address 853 Christchurch Road, Pokesdown BH7 6AR, +44 (0)1202 423408, www.artceterabournemouth.co.uk | **Getting there** Bus 1, 1a, 1b or m2 to Parkwood Road | **Hours** Mon, Tue, Thu & Fri 8.30am–5pm (closed between 1–1.30pm), Sat 8.30am–4.30pm (closed between 1–1.30pm) | **Tip** To get your creative juices flowing, head over the road to Vishuddha Studios & Gallery, which offers art workshops and studio workspace, as well as exhibiting artists' work (www.vishuddhastudios.co.uk).

10 _ The Ashleigh Hotel
The height of his fame

Jo-Jo the Dog-Faced Boy… General Tom Thumb… The Bearded Lady… All were performers in P. T. Barnum's circus in the 19th century. 'The Greatest Showman' employed a menagerie of 'oddities', including Chang the Chinese Giant, who eventually gave up the spotlight to retire to Bournemouth. Described on promotional posters as 'the unquestioned Goliath of the century', he lived at Moyuen (later The Ashleigh Hotel), where he and his wife opened a Chinese teahouse and shop selling Chinese trinkets, silks and teas. At more than eight feet tall, Chang would light his cigar from the gas lamps along the street, and the doorframes and ceilings inside his home were higher than normal to accommodate his lofty frame. Subsequent extensions have been added to the hotel, which highlight just how much more clearance Chang required.

Born Zhan Shichai, his stage name was Chang Woo Gow, which is the name written on the plaque on the front of The Ashleigh Hotel, informing visitors that he lived here from 1890 to 1893. It's believed he moved to Bournemouth to help cure his suspected tuberculosis (see ch. 75), but he died at age 50, supposedly from a broken heart four months after his wife died. Their two teenage sons were taken in by Chang's good friend William James Day, a professional photographer famous for his pictures of Bournemouth and its surroundings. Robert Day, William's father, was the first commercial photographer in Bournemouth, establishing a studio on Lansdowne Road in 1862.

Having lived in the limelight for much of his life, Chang wanted his death to draw no such crowds. He was buried in an eight-and-a-half-foot coffin in an unmarked grave in Wimborne Road Cemetery. That's not to say he doesn't still visit, though. The Ashleigh Hotel's owners are certain that Chang's ghost turns the lights and heating on and off when he sees fit. A tall story? They are adamant it's not.

Address 6 Southcote Road, BH1 3SR, +44 (0)1202 558048, www.ashleighhotel.com | **Getting there** Bus 5a to Unisys, then a 6-minute walk | **Tip** If you're also somewhat sizeable, you may want to check out Big Menswear at 780 Christchurch Road, BH7 6DD, which stocks clothes from sizes L to 8XL.

11 Ashley Walk

A banging place

As you stroll along this stretch of the New Forest, breathing in the fresh air and watching the ponies amble by, ponder the fact that this area wasn't always so tranquil. In fact, between 1940 and 1946, it was downright hectic.

Requisitioned for use as a 5,000-acre bomb training range in World War II, just about every type of air-dropped bomb (with the exception of incendiary devices – imagine the forest fires) was tested here, including the 'bouncing bomb' of Dam Busters fame. The largest bomb ever dropped on British soil exploded here. On 13 March, 1945, the 22,000 lb Grand Slam 'earthquake bomb' – aka Ten Ton Tess – tunnelled into the ground at approximately the speed of sound and left a crater 70 feet deep and 130 feet wide. Given the success of this practice run, 42 Grand Slams were then dropped across Germany to 'encourage' the Nazis to surrender.

Although the Grand Slam crater was filled in after the war, many remain – the Tallboy crater now contains water and resembles a small lake. Other reminders of Ashley Walk's explosive past can also be seen. Like a big pile of chalk used to mark targets on the ground, a large chalk cross, concrete foundations of a 'ship target', an observation shelter (notice the 'V' for victory built into the bricks), the outlines of aircraft pens, and a huge concrete arrow, which would have directed aircraft to an illuminated target in the Lay Gutter valley.

A 'submarine pen' was also constructed here, at a cost of £250,000. Initially believed to be a replica of the shelters Germans used to house their U-boats (hence the 'submarine' nickname), it was later concluded to be a prototype air-raid shelter. Too hefty to remove after the war, it was left standing and covered over with earth. Climb on the top and you'll see concrete peeking through as a result of erosion. You'll also see a wonderful view over the New Forest. Peace is restored.

Address Fordingbridge SP6 2LN | **Getting there** Park in the Ashley Walk Car Park | **Tip** Head to The Fighting Cocks pub, where Ashley Walk personnel were billeted opposite. The outlines of the building bases are still visible.

12 Aubrey Beardsley Mosaic
Shockingly talented

Grotesque… Depraved… Provocative… Looking at this serene scene of a woman smelling grapes, it may surprise you that these words were used to describe many of the works of Victorian artist Aubrey Beardsley, whose 1899 illustration *Autumn* inspired this mosaic. The artwork, located at the site of Beardsley's former home 'Muriel', is a 'sanitised' version; the original is much fruitier – which has nothing to do with the grapes. Three naked women circle the base of the stand, but this is in tame contrast to some of Beardsley's other creations, which depict angry foetuses, severed heads, giant genitalia and, in the case of *Lysistrata Defending the Acropolis*, a stockinged woman delivering a bottom burp into a naked man's face. Charming!

Suffering from tuberculosis, Beardsley moved from London to Bournemouth in 1896, in a bid to let the fresh air ease his ill-health (see ch. 75). It didn't work, and he sadly died from his condition in France at the age of 25. During his short life, with his oft-scandalous black-ink illustrations, this eccentric, controversial artisan was a leading figure – along with his friend Oscar Wilde – in the aesthetic art movement, and contributed significantly to the development of the Art Nouveau style.

His outrageous works inspired local creations, too. Notably the 1979 Poole Pottery Beardsley collection, consisting of 16 ceramic pieces portraying his trademark gasp-inducing figures. The 2011 art project Pride in Bournemouth, which created 50 life-size lions dotted around town, also saw Beardsley celebrated with the monochrome lion named *Aubrey*, who was on display at Castlepoint Shopping Park, before being auctioned for charity.

Described as playful, perverse, sometimes pornographic, whether Beardsley's art leaves you confused, amused, repulsed or titillated, there's no denying his extraordinary imagination and creative gift. It's right there in black and white.

Address Exeter Road, BH2 5DD | Getting there A short walk from Bournemouth Square. The mosaic is on the corner of Terrace Road and Exeter Road, opposite The Odeon. | Tip Beardsley features on the cover of The Beatles' *Sgt. Pepper's Lonely Hearts Club Band* album (second row from the back, far left). Head to Rose Red Records (www.roseredrecords.com) to see if you might be able to spot him.

13 Bailey Bridge
Flat-pack victory

General Eisenhower regarded the Bailey bridge as one of the three most important developments of World War II, along with radar and the heavy bomber aircraft. Field Marshal Montgomery concurred: 'Without the Bailey bridge, we should not have won the war'. A pre-fabricated, portable bridge, the design was conceived by Donald Bailey (later Sir) in 1940; it could be quickly and easily assembled by soldiers preparing the way for fellow troops, equipment, supplies and weapons. Despite the components being lightweight, the bridges were strong enough to hold tanks.

Today, Bailey bridges are still used all over the world, being particularly beneficial in disaster zones, developing countries and as a means of accessing remote regions. And it all started in Christchurch.

This structure located in Stanpit Marsh, spanning Mother Siller's Channel, is the original Bailey bridge, a prototype built following a sketch Bailey had drawn on an envelope.

After this was given the thumbs-up, a 70-foot bridge was soon constructed across the River Stour near the Experimental Bridging Establishment (EBE), on the site of Christchurch Barracks. It took only 36 minutes from the beginning of construction until a lorry could safely drive across.

On Barrack Road (opposite the Bailey Bridge pub) now stands a Bailey bridge panel, with a plaque informing us that, during World War II, 260 miles of the bridge were manufactured. There's also an original panel located in the Red House Museum in Christchurch.

Stanpit Marsh is a beautiful 130-acre nature reserve, and was once owned by Harry Selfridge (of Selfridges department store fame, see ch. 53). It's home to more than 300 species of birds and 300 species of plants – 14 of which are endangered. Visit in late spring to see the newborn foals; watch them graze, completely unaware that they share their patch with a piece of war-winning history.

Address Stanpit Marsh Nature Reserve, Stanpit, Christchurch BH23 3LX | Getting there Bus 1a or X1 to Purewell Cross, then an 8-minute walk to the entrance of Stanpit Marsh. The Bailey bridge is about a 10-minute walk from here. | Tip Not too far from the bridge is a rusty iron lifeboat that once served a US World War II Liberty ship. Used locally in the early 1950s, in 1953 a storm washed it across Priory Marsh to where it sits today.

14 Balmer Lawn Hotel

Flooring it

Do you always do what your boss tells you to? Or do you often disregard instructions and do things your way? If the latter, you'll have something in common with the soldier who stashed top-secret correspondence under the floorboards at the Balmer Lawn Hotel during World War II, rather than burning it, as he'd most certainly have been ordered to do.

In May 2015, during refurbishment work, documents, letters, memos and envelopes stamped 'SECRET' and 'MOST SECRET' were unearthed in Room 10, along with spent bullets, cigarette packs, matchboxes, a soup tin, a toothpaste tube, a rusty razor, a Canadian stamp and *Weekly Illustrated* magazine, dated 25 January, 1936. Inside, an advert for Kensitas cigarettes promised that '1,004 doctors have agreed they are less irritating to the throat than other cigarettes'.

The Balmer Lawn was used as an Army Staff College and the headquarters for the 3rd Canadian Infantry Division (in the garden, a maple tree was planted in memory of all Canadians stationed here in 1944, with a plaque stating: *Their sacrifice will not be forgotten*). Generals Eisenhower and Montgomery met at the hotel to talk D-Day tactics and some of the 'orders of the day' for the invasion were issued from here. A few of the documents found related to D-Day, one detailing the woes of rigging up a 10-mile phone cable as troops advanced into France.

Other papers ranged from 'official and important' (a report of a deserter who tried to flee to Scotland, an envelope addressed to '99 Bomb Disposal', a daily casualty report) to 'day-to-day' (lost-property listings, mess fees, a choir practice reminder). All of this survived a huge fire at the hotel in the 1970s, during which a fireman ran inside to evacuate guests. The manager replied, 'Excuse me, sir, we are partaking in afternoon tea.' Seems the occupant of Room 10 wasn't the only one who had trouble following instructions.

Address Lyndhurst Road, Brockenhurst SO42 7ZB, +44 (0)1590 421040, www.balmerlawnhotel.com | Getting there About a mile from Brockenhurst train station. Along the corridor outside the Club Room on the ground floor is a display of some of the documents found. | Tip Enjoy an alfresco feed in The Lodge Kitchen & Bar. Opened in October 2020 by Eddie 'The Eagle' Edwards, during winter it's decked out as a 'ski lodge', and in the summer it's a 'beach lodge', complete with surfboards, flip-flops and sunglasses hanging from trees, and a life-size Popeye the Sailor Man

15 Beach Hut 2359

Oh, I do like to be beside the seaside

There are around 20,000 beach huts in the UK. Nearly 2,000 are in Bournemouth, where the country's first public beach huts were built in 1909. This one – number 2359 – is the oldest. Designed by borough engineer Frederick Percy Dolamore, the huts (of which 160 were built before World War I) could be hired for £12.10s a year. This would buy you about five Mr Whippys these days. Today, hiring a hut will cost between £1,200 and £2,365 a year (if you ever get to the top of the waiting list – some areas estimate a wait of 18 years!).

The council now owns around 520 of Bournemouth's beach huts; the rest are privately owned. Maintaining its original structural foundations, this seven-foot by seven-foot hut has only needed a few maintenance updates over the years. Its blue plaque was unveiled in 2011 by Jean Smith, who won the Best Kept Beach Hut award the previous year.

As well as the oldest municipal beach hut in the UK, Bournemouth can also boast the most expensive hut. In 2020, one of the 360 beach huts on Mudeford Spit sold for £330,000 (you don't even want to know how many Mr Whippys this would buy you). The average house price in the UK was around £250,000 at the time. The cost of the huts on this idyllic spot/spit has risen hugely over the years; in 1967, one sold for £100, and in the 1980s, one went for £14,500.

Bournemouth's beach huts vary greatly. Some are simple wooden 'sheds', while others are fancy 'surf pods' designed by Wayne and Gerardine Hemingway, who founded fashion label Red or Dead. Another designer to adorn the seafront was Cath Kidston. In the summer of 2015, she decorated five beach huts with her ditsy designs as part of the #RandomActsOfKidston campaign.

Fancy sand in your toes and sunburn on your nose? Why not hire a beach hut – either for a day or the whole summer? Even better, hire number 2359. Deckchairs and hanky hats at the ready.

Address Uncercliff Drive, East Beach, BH1 2EZ, www.bournemouth.co.uk/things-to-do/
beach-hut-hire | Getting there An 8-minute walk from Bournemouth Square through the Lower
Gardens. As you're facing the beach, turn left at Pier Approach and the beach hut is about
500 feet along the prom. | Tip For the full 'British seaside' experience, stop at Harry Ramsden's
just by Pier Approach. With seating for 420 people, it's believed to be one of the largest fish and
chip restaurants in the world (www.harryramsdens.co.uk/location/bournemouth).

16 Bobby's Balconies
Reuse, revive, recycle

In 1986, Bobby Ewing made a comeback in the shower in *Dallas*, having been gone from the hit TV show for a year. Perhaps it's something about the name, but Bobby's department store made a comeback of its own in 2021, having been gone from Bournemouth Square for nearly 50 years.

Established in Margate in 1887 by Frederick Bobby, there were once nine Bobby & Co. stores peppered around the UK – mostly in seaside towns – but, by 1972, they had been taken over by Debenhams. The Bournemouth branch's opening ceremony was hosted by national treasure Terry Wogan.

The 14 original second-floor balconies here – decorated with a 'B' – have remained in situ since 1915, when Bobby's first opened in Bournemouth. New balconies were added to the first-floor windows as part of the recent 'Bobby's Reborn' operation. The copper domes on the roof are another architectural feature of this grand, iconic building that endure from its heyday.

When Debenhams went into liquidation, the fate of the building was uncertain, until Verve Properties – a London company that repurposes buildings that have hit hard times – stepped in. They wanted to bring back the glamour of the shopping experience of yesteryear, with a modern twist. Opening the updated Bobby's in phases, they've really gone to town – with a champagne and sushi bar, ice cream and coffee parlour (with a 'melting point' and 'boiling point'), beauty hall, barber's, art gallery (see ch. 50), market hall, brasserie, bar and rooftop gardens, and Drool, the world's first pop-up food hall dedicated entirely to dogs (there were many wagging tails at the lick 'n' mix station), which was located in the tunnel leading to the Lower Gardens.

Thank goodness these ornate balconies weren't removed or amended with a 'D'. The moral of the story: never get rid of anything (sorry, Marie Kondo) – you never know when you might need it again.

Address Bobby's, Bournemouth Square, BH2 5LY, www.bobbysbournemouth.com | Hours Times vary for individual outlets, so check the website | Tip Also in Bournemouth Square is the *Eternal Flame*, a 15-foot metal stand with a sphere on top. It was originally a naked flame, lit to mark the millennium, but when it was realised it would cost thousands a year to keep it perpetually burning – not to mention the environmental impact – in 2008 it was replaced with an LED globe.

17 Bolton's Bench

Dragon's den

A dragon is a ferocious beast that can't be walked all over. Except, here at Bolton's Bench, it can be. Local folklore says that the hill here isn't a natural knoll but actually the corpse of the Bisterne Dragon, slain in the 15th century by the knight Sir Maurice de Berkeley. Legend has it that the dragon would fly from its lair in Burley Beacon every morning to Bisterne, where locals would give it milk. Berkeley wasn't happy about this so, with his two dogs (named Grim and Holdfast), attacked the dragon – the fight raging throughout the New Forest – until the creature was finally defeated just outside the village of Lyndhurst. The dogs were also killed in the epic tussle.

Although Berkeley was victorious, the encounter left him a broken man who, after 30 days of not eating or sleeping, returned to the site and laid down to die. His yew-wood bow is said to have fallen to the ground beside his body and eventually taken root to grow into one of the six yew trees that can still be seen today on top of the hill/dragon. There are stone carvings of the dragon and two dogs on Bisterne Manor, and there's a Dragon Field at Lower Bisterne Farm, which is where a large part of the battle supposedly took place. There's also the Green Dragon pub at Brook, about six miles from Bolton's Bench.

Another local dragon tale is that of the five-headed Christchurch Dragon, which is said to have burned down the town in 1113. Witnessed by nine French canons visiting the area, the building in which they had been offered a bed for the night miraculously remained uncharred. In 2013, to mark the 900th anniversary of the story, locals hosted the Christchurch Dragon Festival. The event made some noise, with the 'heartbeat' of the dragon being pounded out during the drumming event at Druitt Hall. Thankfully, the beast didn't return to finish the place off with its fiery breath.

Address Beaulieu Road, Lyndhurst SO43 7NL | **Getting there** About 2.5 miles from Ashurst New Forest train station | **Tip** Walk down the hill, past the cricket pavilion, and you'll see a water trough on your right. The plaque reads: *In grateful and reverent memory of all horses and other creatures who have given their lives in the service of man throughout the ages.*

18 Bookends

Piece it all together

The word 'jigsaw' gives you 17 points in Scrabble. 'Puzzle' gives you 26. As you're browsing the 400-plus jigsaw puzzles that Bookends stocks, take a moment to consider that, from 1927 to 1988, hundreds of thousands of jigsaws were produced at a factory on Palmerston Road in Boscombe.

Having developed his own jigsaws out of calendar pictures and scraps of plywood in his shed, Gerald Hayter quit his job as a bank clerk and founded G. J. Hayter & Co. Ltd, which produced the popular, hand-cut Victory jigsaw puzzles, a favourite with the late Queen Mother. In 1970, the company was bought out by board game manufacturer Spear's Games, which was taken over by Mattel in 1994. Mattel is now a multinational, owning more than 235 brands, including Fisher-Price, Barbie, Hot Wheels and… Scrabble.

Another local toy factory of days gone by was Forest Toys in Brockenhurst. Set up by artist and wood-carver Frank Whittington (a relative of the real Dick Whittington) in 1922, the Noah's Arks and zoo sets became particularly popular. After Queen Mary ordered two dozen Arks on the spot, they were soon stocked in Harrods and Selfridges. In the late 1930s, Frank carved a trio of musicians from the Bournemouth Symphony Orchestra performing in a concert at the Balmer Lawn Hotel (see ch. 14). The piece is now in storage at the Russell-Cotes Museum (see ch. 67) and can be viewed by appointment.

You can buy Scrabble from Bookends, along with a *Scrabble Secrets* book, which suggests maximising points with minimal tiles with words like 'za' (short for pizza – yes, it's allowed!). Among the well-known jigsaw brands – Ravensburger, Falcon, Jumbo – the independent shop also stocks an exclusive range of jigsaws featuring local scenes, such as the Red Arrows over the pier, Hengistbury Head beach huts and Christchurch Priory at sunrise, photographed by Roger Holman. How many points does 'wowsers' get?

Address 67 High Street, Christchurch BH23 1AU, +44 (0)1202 479059, www.bookendsonline.co.uk | **Getting there** Bus 1a to Christchurch town centre | **Hours** Mon–Sat 9am–5.30pm, Sun 11am–4.30pm | **Tip** Another independent shop on Christchurch's high street is Eden Boutique (www.facebook.com/edenchristchurch), selling a range of lovely fashion pieces, accessories, gifts and homeware. No jigsaws, though.

19 Boscombe Devil
Giving revellers the evil eye

Have you had a night out in the venue opposite this effigy of Satan? Depending on your age, you may have watched Laurel and Hardy perform there in 1947, Rod Stewart in 1971 or Ed Sheeran in 2011. But on your arrival and departure, were you aware that you were being watched – perhaps cursed – by Old Nick?

Believed to have been put in place by the Plymouth Brethren or the Lord's Day Observance Society, puritans were incensed that the theatre was open on a Sunday, and would kneel outside to pray for the spiritual welfare of the performers and audiences. No longer visible, the original inscription next to the hellish figure read: *The devil comes into his own.*

A series of other carved devils used to sit on the verandah and roof, holding shields to protect themselves from the risqué performances taking place opposite, but they are now gone. Owners of the venue grew so concerned about entering the building on a Sunday that they constructed the face of an angel – which can still be seen – on the ceiling of the main auditorium to 'counteract' any curses the devils may have inflicted on them, and to reassure visitors that 'all was forgiven'.

The Grand Pavilion Theatre was constructed in 1895 and has changed hands – and names – many times. It has served as a theatre, a circus (see ch. 40), a cinema, a ballroom, a nightclub, and is now the live-entertainment venue O2 Academy Bournemouth. Over the years, the disapproving devil has had much 'immorality' to scowl at – from the American-style glamour revues featuring tableaux of nude ladies behind screens at Boscombe Hippodrome during World War II, to the Miss England beauty contests held at Tiffany's disco in the 1970s, to the '£1 a tequila shot' days of the 1990s at the Opera House nightclub. Not to mention the murdering of various songs in the first karaoke bar in the UK in the Academy nightclub. Wicked fun.

Address 583 Christchurch Road, Boscombe BH1 4AN | Getting there Bus 1, 1a or m2 to Palmerston Road | Tip Another addition to the precinct intended to deter bad behaviour is the Tardis-style police box, added in 2014, much to the delight of Dr Who fans.

20 Bournemouth School
An education for heroes and villains

Established in 1901, Bournemouth School's alumni list reads like a who's who of the rich and famous. Rugby player Charlie Ewels, choirmaster Gareth Malone and bass player of Blur Alex James were all educated here. But perhaps the most notable former students were Batman and Blofeld. Or, to give them their real names, Christian Bale and Charles Gray.

Now a Hollywood star with more than 50 movies under his (utility) belt – including *The Dark Knight* trilogy – Christian Bale spent much of his childhood in Bournemouth. Between 1985 and 1991, he lived on Capstone Road and skated at Westover Ice Rink. At age 11, he landed the starring role in Stephen Spielberg's *Empire of the Sun*. He took half a year off school to make the film and ultimately left Bournemouth School at 16. He moved to America with his dad (following his parents' divorce) a year later. His mum and one of his three sisters still live in Bournemouth.

Charles Gray – best known as the villainous, chair-swivelling, feline-stroking Blofeld in James Bond's *Diamonds Are Forever* – attended Bournemouth School in the mid-1940s. At the same time, comedian Benny Hill – who'd been evacuated from Southampton to Bournemouth due to the war – was educated in the same building, as part of Taunton's School. Gray grew up at 7 Howard Road, where his parents remained until their death. He worked at Rebbeck Brothers estate agents in Bournemouth Square and trod the boards at Bournemouth Little Theatre, before leaving town in the late 1950s.

Besides educating film stars, Bournemouth School had a more vital role during World War II. In 1940, 1,000-plus French soldiers evacuated from Dunkirk were billeted here, then 400 British soldiers rescued from Cherbourg. Classrooms were used as a hospital for those wounded. 'Batman' may have been in attendance decades later but, during this time, the school offered refuge to real-life heroes.

Address East Way, BH8 9PY, +44 (0)1202 512609, www.bournemouth-school.org | Getting there Bus m1 or 3 to St Francis Church | Hours Viewable from the outside only | Tip Bournemouth School for Girls has also produced some acting talent, including *Peaky Blinders*' Sophie Rundle, *Call the Midwife*'s Victoria Yeates, and *Hollyoaks* actresses Beth Kingston and Tamaryn Payne.

21 Bournemouth Scout Museum

Be prepared

Are you: honourable, trustworthy, loyal, helpful, a friend to animals, obedient, thrifty and do you smile and whistle under all difficulties? If so, you'd make a great Scout. The Scout Law – which incorporates the above attributes – was written by Lord Robert Baden-Powell, the founder of the Scouts, in 1908. It has been etched into a wooden panel and is hanging in this museum.

One person who made a great Scout was Arthur Primmer, one of the 20 boys to attend Baden-Powell's 'experimental camp' on Brownsea Island (10 miles away), from 1 – 9 August, 1907, which launched the worldwide Scout movement. Today, there are more than 50 million Scouts in 216 countries. In Uganda, Scouts supported nurses in rolling out a measles vaccination programme in the early 1990s, just after the AIDs crisis had brought it to a halt. In Iceland, Scouts provide mountain-rescue services. It's no exaggeration to say that Baden-Powell's camp changed people's lives and the world. Arthur's shirt is displayed here, with other Scout uniforms through the ages.

You'll also find much Scouting memorabilia. Don't be alarmed when you come to a golden 'thanks badge' in the shape of a swastika. Prior to the Nazis using it as a symbol of hate, the 'swastika' was actually known as a 'fylfot' and represented gratitude and luck. In 1934, Baden-Powell stopped using this symbol due to its negative connotations.

The museum houses many books too, including various editions of the handbook *Scouting for Boys* by Baden-Powell, first published in 1908. It has sold more than 100 million copies globally, making it one of the best-selling books of all time. The aforementioned Scout Law was written for inclusion in the first *Scouting for Boys* manual. The 10th instruction – 'A scout is clean in thought, word and deed' – was added in 1911. Still think you'd make a good Scout?

Address Butchers Coppice Scout Camp, Holloway Avenue, BH11 9JW, +44 (0)1202 574747, bookings@butcherscoppice.org.uk, www.butcherscoppice.org.uk | **Getting there** Bus 5 or 5a to Poole Lane, then a 10-minute walk | **Hours** The museum is open by appointment only; phone or email to arrange a visit | **Tip** The museum is part of the seven-and-a-half-acre activity centre Butchers Coppice, which is said to have a resident ghost – an 18th-century smuggler buried alive. Between the copse and where the toilet block now stands, one of the tunnels used to smuggle contraband ended, and had to be filled in quickly as customs officers approached. The doomed man was still inside.

22 Bronze Age Barrow
How do you like them apples?

What do you see? A collection of shrubs and brambles in the middle of a residential area, right? Well, it's what you can't see that makes this site – a burial ground from the Bronze Age, around 4,000 years ago – interesting. Beneath the foliage, underground, are the remains of local people buried here. Located in the Friars Cliff neighbourhood, this is just one of Dorset's 2,000 tumuli (barrows, or burial grounds), with many others dotted around locally.

While a lot of barrows have been destroyed to make room for housing and other infrastructure, many remain. Among others, there are 31 at Oakley Down near Cranborne, 23 at Nine Barrow Down in the Purbecks (perhaps they named the area before they'd finished counting), 13 at Hengistbury Head, 11 at St Catherine's Hill (see ch. 94) and two on Kinson Common. You'll also find a plinth in West Cliff Gardens, on the site of a Bronze Age barrow, put in place by Westbourne Rotary Club in 2005 to celebrate its centenary.

One of the barrows at Hengistbury Head is of international significance. Excavations on the old pitch and putt course in 2001 revealed an urn containing cremated human bones and crab apples. Thought to be part of a symbolic ritual offering, this was only the second time that crab apples had been found in such a scenario in northwest Europe, which caused much interest in the worldwide archaeology community. The carbonised crab apples are on display in the Hengistbury Head visitor centre (and apple pie is served at the Hiker Café there).

When Friars Cliff was developed in the 1930s, pieces of Bronze Age pottery were found on Seaway Avenue and Bure Lane, with arrowheads also found in the area, one from the Neolithic period (10,000 B.C. to 3,000 B.C.). The barrow here is nationally important, and is listed under the Ancient Monuments and Archaeological Areas Act 1979.

Much more than a collection of shrubs and brambles after all.

Address Glengarry Way, Friars Cliff, Christchurch BH23 4EH | Getting there Bus 1a to Somerford Hotel, then a 20-minute walk. About 2.5 miles from Hinton Admiral train station. The barrow is opposite Vecta Close. | Tip In Hengistbury Head visitor centre, pick up details of how to navigate the area's Archaeology Trail, which takes you back in time through the Stone, Bronze and Iron Ages.

23 Centre VR
A whole new world

How do you fancy swimming with a whale, attacking a zombie and shooting lasers in outer space all in one day? Or throwing a stapler at your boss, standing beside the Pyramids and sparring with Rocky Balboa? At Centre VR, Europe's largest virtual reality venue, you can do all these things… and more. With over 150 titles – in categories including sport, experience, flying, shooter, horror, battle, puzzle and escape room – you can enter almost any kind of virtual-reality scenario imaginable. You'll be hooked up to a headset, asked to hold a controller in each hand, then set loose in a new world. Job Simulator is by far the most popular title, with 53,822 minutes being played over a 12-month period in 2019 and 2020 – which accounted for more than a quarter of the centre's total play time. The goofy game requires the player to become either a gourmet chef, mechanic, store clerk or office worker, and is then encouraged to wreak havoc in their workplace.

Google Earth is also a popular title, which allows visitors to explore the world from a new perspective. With its 'fly' function, you can satisfy your wanderlust by soaring over the Grand Canyon, coming face to face with Christ the Redeemer or simply zooming down your own street. Tower Tag – a multiplayer laser-tag game – is also great fun, and popular for parties. Each player wears a jacket that vibrates whenever they're hit, while they try to conquer as many towers as possible. Bring your best shot.

If freaking yourself out is more your speed, try Richie's Plank Experience, in which you're 80 storeys high and standing in front of a plank. It's amazing how your body reacts as if you're actually *there*. Knees knocking and palms sweating, will you bottle it or inch out over the city below? Don't look down!

Wherever you choose to venture, it'll be an experience unlike any you've ever had before. Virtually.

Address Richmond Gardens Shopping Centre, Old Christchurch Road, BH1 1EP, +44 (0)1202 878300, www.centrevr.co.uk | **Getting there** A 5-minute walk from Bournemouth Square | **Hours** Times can vary so check the website, but these are the usual hours. Term-time: Thu & Fri noon–11pm, Sat & Sun 10am–11pm. School holidays: Mon–Wed 10am–8pm, Thu–Sun 10am–11pm | **Tip** For even more virtual-reality games, visit The Lockey Escape Rooms at 2 Yelverton Road, BH1 1DF and 35 The Triangle, BH2 5SE (www.thelockey.com).

24 Chaplin's

A melting pot of eccentricity

'A day without laughter is a day wasted' – Charlie Chaplin. This quote above an Art-Deco-style mural of the silent-movie star may be the first thing you see when you enter this boozer. But such is the nature of the eclectic decor, you may miss it entirely, your eyes being drawn to the stained-glass windows, clocks, photos, paintings, figurines, mugs, jugs, vases, mirrors… and other Charlie Chaplin memorabilia. Not to mention the TV above the bar screening some of his movies – *The Vagabond, City Lights, Modern Times…*

Modern Times – one of the many films Chaplin wrote, directed, produced and starred in – is the name of the venue's latest addition, a restaurant serving classic British dishes (fish and chips, shepherd's pie, Sunday roasts) with a modern twist. Artist Vivien Hoffman has bedecked the bright, playful eatery with 100 artworks of Chaplin, all painted in a different style – many a homage to renowned artists like Van Gogh, Picasso and Da Vinci. Can you spot Chaplin as the Vitruvian Man or in the Café Terrace at Night?

Although a worldwide icon, Chaplin had a local connection. Fred Karno, the man who launched the actor's career – and who invented the custard-pie-in-the-face gag – moved to Poole in his later years and bought an off-licence (with financial help from Chaplin) at 296 Sandbanks Road. When Karno died in 1941, Chaplin sent a wreath to his funeral at Bournemouth Crematorium.

Like the Hollywood star, Chaplin's is no stranger to an acceptance speech, having scooped awards such as UK's Best Pub for Entertainment, Best Community Pub and Britain's Best Beer Garden. The giant face painted on the garden wall is that of owner Harry Seccombe, always watching to check his patrons are having fun. Good times are encouraged, with punny signs dotted around, including the suit of armour that states: *Always a good knight at Chaplin's*. After all, a day without laughter is a day wasted.

Address 529 Christchurch Road, Boscombe BH1 4AG, +44 (0)1202 251953, www.chaplins-bar.co.uk | Getting there Bus 1, 1a or m2 to Boscombe Crescent | Hours Check the website as opening hours vary | Tip Venture downstairs to The Cellar Bar, which hosts comedy nights, theatre productions, poetry readings and live music. You may even get to enjoy an impromptu gig from artists playing at the nearby O2 Academy Bournemouth. Such was the case in 2015 when Alabama 3 – of *The Sopranos* theme-tune fame – jammed here.

25 Charles Bennett's Grave
Golden boy

Mo Farah… Kelly Holmes… Linford Christie… Sally Gunnell… All British Olympic gold medallists. Add to the list Charles Bennett, who was the first British track and field athlete to become an Olympic champion. He won two gold medals (for the 1,500 metres and 5,000 metres) and a silver (in the steeplechase) at the Paris Olympics in 1900, also smashing the 1,500-metre world record. On returning home, he was carried shoulder-high through the streets of Wimborne in celebration.

However, he had been all but forgotten for many years… until 2000, when his grandson went on a mission to uncover his 'hidden grave'. Armed with a map of St Andrew's churchyard, some shears and a garden fork, Chris Bennett unearthed his grandfather's gravestone, which was in a sorry state. Local stonemason Anthony Ives Memorials donated this headstone, an altogether more fitting memorial for a man who made history.

Nicknamed the Shapwick Express, Charles grew up in the village of Shapwick in Dorset. He was a steam train driver, operating the Bournemouth to Waterloo line. Today, the villagers host races every Olympic year to honour their local hero. The tradition began in 2000 with the Charles Bennett Millennium Mile Race, which saw a runner dressed as Bennett carrying a replica of the Olympic torch through the village. Fellow record-breaking athlete Sydney 'The Mighty Atom' Wooderson even came from his Wareham home to watch the race. Four years later, using funds raised from the event, the Charles Bennett Village Green was opened.

Another local British Olympian to be honoured for his gold-medal achievement is Ben Ainslie. On Lymington's High Street, a postbox was painted gold by Royal Mail to celebrate Ainslie sailing his way to victory in the Men's Heavyweight Dinghy event.

Ready to visit the gravestone? On your marks, get set… GO!

Address St Andrew's Church, Millhams Road, Kinson BH10 7LN, +44 (0)1202 570010, www.standrewskinson.org | Getting there Bus 5 or 5a to The Kinson Hub, then a 4-minute walk. Go past the church and the red-brick building, keep to the right of the graveyard and walk to the end, turn left and the grave is the sixth one in. | Tip The houses at Bournemouth's oldest school, Kinson Academy, are called Gulliver, Fryer, Ward and Bennett, named after local historical figures: smuggler Isaac Gulliver (see ch. 55), landowners Elizabeth and William Fryer, long-standing headmistress Lilian Ward, and Charles Bennett.

26 __ Chewton Glen Beehives
Positively buzzing

Chewton Glen is more than a five-star hotel with Lamborghinis often parked out front and £3,610 bottles of champagne on the menu. It's also an ecosystem unto itself. Having introduced five beehives onto the 130-acre estate in 2010, there are now 70, each containing between 30,000 and 60,000 buzzing beauties. Queen bees for each hive had historically been purchased from Denmark but, with the sting of Brexit, 'plan B(ee)' was implemented: rearing queen bees onsite.

Wander around the impressive grounds in spring and summer and you'll notice that many of the flowers are on the blue spectrum. Bees are attracted to this hue as their eyes are most sensitive to it, so when estate manager Darren Venables is dreaming up the hotel's colour scheme each season, he takes this into consideration to maximise pollination. He also considers which vegetables, herbs and edible flowers to grow for the cookery school The Kitchen, which is led by celebrity chef James Martin.

Homegrown ingredients used in the hotel's main restaurant, The Dining Room, include lemon verbena, concocted into a zingy sorbet palate cleanser, and cucamelons, eaten as bar snacks (much fancier than peanuts). And guess where the honey for the iced honeycomb parfait comes from? Yep! You can also sample Chewton Glen honey in a smoothie at the spa, in a hot toddy at the bar, and from the boutique in a jar. Jars of jams, jellies and chutneys are also produced using the fruit foraged from the two orchards here, and sold under the Naked Jams brand, which supplies The Ritz London.

As well as the working beehives stretched across three apiaries, you'll also find The Beehive children's club, housed in a fun 'den' in the woods, complete with giant bee door knocker, bee cupboard door handles and bee cushions. The resident insects swarm to the Bug Hotel and make themselves comfortable. You won't find any Lamborghinis out front here though.

Address Chewton Glen Hotel & Spa, Christchurch Road, New Milton BH25 6QS, +44 (0)1425 275341, www.chewtonglen.com | Getting there Bus X2 or 1a to Milestone Roundabout, then a 12-minute walk. Less than 2 miles from New Milton train station. There's also a helipad! | Tip Just up the road, you'll find café and deli Two Bees by the Sea (www.twobeesbythesea.co.uk).

27 The Chine Hotel
Remembering the variety pack

Oliver Hardy's famous catchphrase 'Well, here's another nice mess [often misquoted as "another fine mess"] you've gotten me into!' could have been tweaked to 'Well, here's another nice *hotel* you've gotten me into!' when he and comedy partner Stan Laurel stayed at The Chine Hotel during their UK tour in August 1947. Performing twice-nightly for a week at Boscombe's Hippodrome (now O2 Academy Bournemouth), they left their mark at the hotel, in the form of black-and-white photos now proudly displayed. In one, they're wearing chef's hats in the hotel kitchen, and one is signed, 'Thanks for the lovely visit Fred & Wanda'.

Fred Butterworth didn't just count this slapstick duo among his friends. As well as The Chine Hotel and Hippodrome, he also owned 17 other theatres all over the country, including Richmond Theatre in London. He hired the likes of Norman Wisdom, Morecambe and Wise, Arthur Lucan (aka Old Mother Riley) and Fred Karno (the man who 'discovered' Charlie Chaplin – see ch. 24) to entertain audiences, often in-between films being screened. These famous faces – as well as dozens more from the heyday of variety theatre in the 1940s, 1950s and 1960s – are displayed alongside Laurel and Hardy's, most autographed with personal messages to Fred – or 'F. J. Butterworth'.

Fred passed away in 1984, and O2 Academy Bournemouth and Richmond Theatre are now owned by Fred's son, John, along with The Chine Hotel and other local FJB Hotels: Haven Hotel, Harbour Heights Hotel and Sandbanks Hotel. John has fond childhood memories of meeting stars at The Chine, such as Vera Lynn and Diana Dors. Although he doesn't remember it being taken, he has a photo of Laurel and Hardy posing on the hotel's steps while holding him as a baby. Luckily, he's not crying, being sick or making any deposits into his nappy, or you can just imagine Hardy muttering, 'Well, here's another nice mess…'.

Address 25 Boscombe Spa Road, Boscombe BH5 1AX, +44 (0)800 484 0048, www.fjbhotels.co.uk/chine-hotel | Getting there Bus 1a to Boscombe Gardens, then a 6-minute walk. The photo display is on the lower-ground floor. | Hours The hotel is open Mar–Oct | Tip From the Gallery Bar & Brasserie, look out over the three acres of gardens, home to a beautiful 160-year-old pine tree. Pictures of various stars are hung in here too – including Cliff Richard, Elizabeth Taylor and, again, Laurel and Hardy.

28 Christine Keeler's Pad

Painting the town pink

It was the scandal that gripped the nation. And, before the 19-year-old woman at the centre of it was thrust into the limelight, she visited Bournemouth with her friend. Christine Keeler and Mandy Rice-Davies rented the top-floor flat at 54 East Avenue in Talbot Woods in May 1962, a few months after war secretary John Profumo and Christine had ended their illicit liaison – the now-famous Profumo Affair. In March 1963, Profumo denied the dalliance in parliament but was forced to admit he was lying, and ultimately resigned. The scandal is said to have brought down the British government.

When Christine and Mandy arrived at the flat, they pretended they were married – giving the names Mrs Christine Pringle and Mrs Mandy Webb – and had their 'husbands' in tow. Landlady Marjorie Wall recalled that Christine covered her bedroom walls with nude photos of herself, and that the group would party all night. Christine and Mandy would visit El Cabala coffee bar on Old Christchurch Road (now NM Money), Swiss Restaurant on Bourne Avenue (now Moose Kitchen – see ch. 64) and Raymond hair salon, run by Raymond Bessone, aka Mr Teazie Weazie, who was Britain's first celebrity hairdresser. Keeler became known around town as 'the girl in pink jeans'.

After the women left the flat, Marjorie found letters hidden in drawers and under the carpet that she later sent to Lord Denning for his inquiry into the scandal.

Another person embroiled in the Profumo Affair was osteopath Dr Stephen Ward. A socialite, he had introduced Christine and Mandy to many rich, powerful men and was eventually accused of living off the women's 'immoral earnings'. Ward had local connections, being educated at Canford School in Wimborne, graduating in 1929, and later being stationed at Bovington Camp during World War II. He took a fatal overdose the night before the jury found him guilty. A sorry affair.

Address 54 East Avenue, Winton BH3 7DA | Getting there Bus 6 to Talbot Roundabout, then a 12-minute walk | Hours Viewable from the outside only | Tip Ossemsley Manor in Christchurch used to house the nightclub said to have been frequented by Christine Keeler and John Profumo.

29 Conker Spirit Tour
Find your gin-spiration

A word to the wise: if you're planning to take a Conker Spirit distillery tour, don't drive. Between the gin and tonic you'll receive on arrival to the tasting samples of the seven spirits the company produces, to the espresso martini served as a buzz-inducing finale to the evening, you'll most certainly be too sloshed to get behind the wheel. The tour is hosted by 'Head Conkerer' Rupert Holloway, who quit his job as a chartered surveyor in 2014 to follow his gin passion. He set up Dorset's first distillery, which now produces 1,200 bottles of his signature Dorset Dry Gin every week.

For six months, Rupert had mixed, blended, distilled and – along with his willing friends and family – tasted his 'conkoctions'. With Recipe 38, he landed on the perfect combination of 10 botanicals, two of which are locally sourced: marsh samphire and gorse flowers. Every spring, a Conker team heads to the New Forest to forage for gorse; they collect enough to last a year, drying and vacuum-packing it to preserve its sweet flavour. New Forest Spring Water is used to distil the spirit.

Before the Conker distillery moved to Southbourne in 2015, production began in a small terraced house in Christchurch that Rupert was renting at the time (he had a very understanding landlord). The coordinates of this house are on the bottle's label. Although Conker is stocked in hundreds of bars, pubs, restaurants and shops up and down the UK, home is where its heart is, and Rupert sticks to his roots wherever possible. The bottle labels are printed by Labelwell in Christchurch; the coffee beans used in the Cold Brew Coffee Liqueur, although sourced from Brazil and Ethiopia, are roasted by Dorset-based Beanpress; and for every 70cl bottle of the Navy Strength Gin sold, £5 is donated to the RNLI (Royal National Lifeboat Institution), which has its headquarters in Poole. A real community spirit.

Address 16a Inverleigh Road, Southbourne BH6 5HA, +44 (0)1202 430384, www.conkerspirit.co.uk | Getting there Bus 1b to Burleigh Road, then a 5-minute walk | Hours Tours are run on Thursdays from 7–9pm, booking essential (check the website for dates) | Tip Conker Port Barrel Gin label displays the coordinates of the Douro Valley in Portugal where the port barrels are obtained; the Cold Brew Coffee Liqueur has the coordinates of where it's brewed (the Conker headquarters); and the RNLI Navy Strength Gin displays the coordinates of the charity's HQ where you can grab a drink with a view in the Slipway Bar.

30 The Cookie Shack

Hundreds and thousands of biscuits

With her jaunty felt-biscuit hat (complete with mini deckchair), pet dog named Rosé (after the wine), and 'All the biscuity best' email sign off, Sarah Bates is anything but cookie-cutter. Which is ironic, given her profession and the fact that she makes around 1,000 biscuits a month, using her 300-plus cutters.

Having quit her job as a primary school teacher in 2014, Sarah got bitten by the biscuit bug after making a batch as favours for her brother-in-law's wedding. She enrolled in courses with Penningtons School of Cake Artistry and WSX Enterprise, read *Brilliant Biscuits* by Pamela Giles cover to cover, then set up her business, Biscuits by Sarah B. What a smart cookie! For a while, she hosted 'Calm Cookie-ing' sessions at Urban Shanti Community Studio in Boscombe.

Sarah continues to delight wedding guests with her crumbly creations, like the Mini Coopers with the couple's surname on the number plate, and the sausage dogs carried in the bride's hand luggage to a wedding in Las Vegas. Sarah also caters for birthdays, other special occasions, and corporate events, for the likes of Castlepoint, Topshop and South Coast Makers Market. There's no shape she won't try, having crafted everything from Yoda to mermaids, ketchup bottles to a chilled-out woman with a face mask on. She also runs biscuit-decorating classes and parties, either out and about or in The Cookie Shack at the end of her garden.

Previously a shed, the space was converted by Sarah's builder neighbour during the Covid lockdowns of 2020 into an all-singing, all-baking outhouse, complete with two ovens, a sink with running water, two workstations, two dehydrators to speed up the icing-drying process, and enough space to house her 50 varieties of sprinkles.

Got sprinkle envy? Join The Shire Bakery's Sprinkle Club subscription service. You could also indulge in some edible glitter sprays – or, as Sarah calls them, 'fairy farts'.

Address 15 Droxford Road, BH6 5PL, www.biscuitsbysarahb.co.uk | Getting there Bus 1a to Harewood Avenue; about half a mile from Pokesdown train station | Hours Check the website for details of class times | Tip The East Street Deli in Wimborne and Fordingbridge Farm Shop stock Sarah's biscuits – some in the shape of cheese.

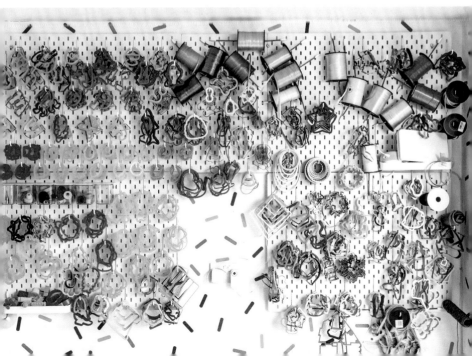

31_Coty
Are you ready for your close-up?

'You are not born glamorous. Glamour is created.' So said Polish make-up artist Max Factor, who became Hollywood's go-to guy for beautifying starlets such as Ava Gardner, Jean Harlow and Judy Garland. In 1928, he won an Oscar for his contributions to the film industry. Factor coined the term 'make-up' and, not only did he create glamour for the silver screen, he also created glamour for the everywoman, with his inventions of Pan-Cake foundation, Lip Pomade (later called lip gloss), Erace concealer and the wand mascara.

From 1947 to 1994, Max Factor products were manufactured in Bournemouth and exported all over the globe from this site, where Coty's distribution centre and offices now stand. Coty is one of the world's largest beauty companies and owns around 80 brands, including Max Factor. The two Max Factor factories on Francis Avenue had previously been used to manufacture radar sets for aircraft during the war (they have now been demolished and housing built in their place). One factory would turn out 'wet' cosmetics such as skin cream, face lotion, foundation, cream rouge, lipstick and mascara. The other made 'dry' items including face powder, compact rouge and Pan-Cake make-up. Up to 12,000 lipsticks, 12,000 boxes of face powder, 90,000 rouge compacts and 140,000 Pan-Cake compacts were produced each day.

Workers – who may have been doing anything from stamping 'MF' onto lipstick cases to dropping tiny balls into nail varnishes – could buy a 'lucky dip' bag of various make-up items for next to nothing. Such was the take-up of these bargain beauty buys that Bournemouth department stores closed their Max Factor counters in the 1970s as so many people had friends/family who could provide cosmetics on the cheap (at one time, the only shop in town that stocked Max Factor was Boots). Those who snagged cut-price concealer and low-cost lippy were made up.

Address Wallisdown Road, BH11 8PL, +44 (0)1202 635400, www.coty.com, www.maxfactor.com/en-gb | **Getting there** About 2.5 miles from Branksome train station | **Hours** Viewable from the outside only | **Tip** Look across the road and you'll see a building with a lion perched on top. This 1930 premises was previously used by social-justice charity Nacro, but is now independent specialist school The Lion Works School (www.thelionworksschool.org).

32 A Coven of Witches

Double, double, toil and trouble

Burley village in the New Forest is a magical place. Not just because of its quaint tea rooms, thatched cottages or the roaming ponies, but because of its connection to witchcraft. In the late 1950s, Burley was home to Sybil Leek, the first person in Britain to proclaim herself a white witch after the Witchcraft Act was repealed in 1951. She'd walk around in a black cloak with her pet jackdaw, named Mr Hotfoot Jackson, on her shoulder (and sometimes head!). During World War II, Sybil was recruited by the British government to provide phony horoscopes to the Germans. She apparently convinced Hitler's deputy, Rudolf Hess, to fly to Scotland, where he was captured. Sybil was the high priestess of the Horsa coven in the New Forest, which still has a following today. She promoted white witchery in her books and on TV, and became 'Britain's most famous witch'. So famous, in fact, that visitors flocked to Burley to get in on the action. Residents weren't enchanted.

In 1964, Sybil moved to the US, but not before naming this shop, A Coven of Witches, which sells everything from wands to dreamcatchers, crystals to bumper stickers declaring 'My Other Car is a Broom'. While you're there, sign up for a witchcraft workshop, get a psychic reading or encounter the ghost of a cat who used up its nine lives, and apparently graces the shop with its purring presence. You can also look at the old photos of Sybil and her jackdaw by the fireplace. And don't miss the terracotta dragon perched atop the shop. A local piece of folklore states that, at Burley Beacon, a dragon lived in its lair (see ch. 17).

Sybil wasn't the only local famous advocate of the occult. Gerald Brosseau Gardener, recognised as the founder of modern paganism, lived in Highcliffe, and a blue plaque adorns his former home at 3 Highland Avenue, celebrating him as the 'Father of Modern Witchcraft'. Spellbinding stuff.

Address The Cross, Burley, Ringwood BH24 4AA, +44 (0)1425 402449, www.covenofwitches.co.uk | Getting there By car, take Wessex Way, A338, A31, Ringwood Road, then a slight left onto The Cross | Hours Daily 10am–5pm | Tip Just around the corner is Witchcraft, another shop specialising in witchy wonders (5 The Mall, BH24 4BS).

33 The Cricketers

Howzat!

If you saw a fight break out in a pub, you might assume that those throwing punches had had a few too many. If, however, you saw two men coming to blows here in the 1970s and 1980s, you would have been witnessing training sessions in the Freddie Mills Boxing Gymnasium. The Bournemouth-born boxing champ (see ch. 46) lived on nearby Spring Road and would drink here. After his death, the gym was opened in his name. Its sign is hung in the raised area of the pub, where the gym once stood.

From boxing rings to wedding rings, prior to this – in the early 1900s – the pub was used as a chapel on Sundays. There's a black and white photo hung in the Private Bar (as opposed to the Public Bar – the etched windows label the rooms as such) showing five members of a bridal party posing in front of the ornate Victorian fireplace. Note the decorative cast-iron air vents dotted around the room, which would serve as receptacles for love notes/rendezvous requests for members of the congregation courting on the sly.

Established in 1847, The Cricketers (previously The Cricketers Hotel, then The Cricketers Arms) is the oldest pub in Bournemouth and was so-named due to the cricket ground that stood opposite the building. It has maintained many of its original fittings, including the mahogany doors in the Public Bar and the men's urinals, which are surprisingly attractive – with their black and white mosaic tiling – given their function.

The wooden bar originates from a cruise liner, which gives this 'proper locals' pub' somewhat of an 'international edge', not least because there are hundreds of foreign banknotes stuck to it. The tradition of accepting unused currency from regulars returning from their hols began with two halves of a £10 note, belonging to a pair of friends who wanted to 'join forces' to buy a round ('Make mine a half!'). One part of this note is displayed on the left side of the main bar.

Address 41 Windham Road, Boscombe BH1 4RN, +44 (0)1202 551589 | Getting there Bus 2 to Ophir Gardens, then a 5-minute walk | **Hours** Mon–Thu 11am–11pm, Fri & Sat 11am–11.30pm, Sun noon–10.30pm | **Tip** At the junction of Shelbourne Close and Holdenhurst Road, you'll find another old noteworthy toilet. Now a Grade II-listed building – complete with domed roof and Crittall windows – the early-1900s structure was used as a gents' public loo until 2017.

34 Dome Skylight
Looking shipshape

As you're browsing the clothes in Fat Face, take a moment to look up. You may find that you forget all about locating the fitting room and become captivated by the wrought-iron and glass dome skylight. Now surrounded by a colourful sea-themed mural, it has been the focal point of the building for the past century.

Built in the 1920s, the first business to occupy these premises was Cadena Café, which served food and fancies by waitresses in frilly pinafores. Since then, the building has been Dillons Bookshop, Athena, Pilot Clothing and The Other Place nightclub. It is now casual-clothing shop Fat Face.

The intricate dome looks almost identical to the ones on the RMS *Mauretania* ocean liner, the world's largest ship until 1910. Described as a 'floating palace', when it hung up its foghorn in 1934, all of the furnishings, fittings and fixtures – including the seven dome skylights – were auctioned off at Southampton Docks. The auction consisted of 3,503 lots (everything from the lifeboats to the captain's cushions were up for grabs) and lasted eight days.

Mr Tom Cullen, who was a big fan of travelling on the transatlantic vessel, purchased the interior of the second-class drawing room and the officers' cabins, which he installed in his white and blue beach villa, The Boat House, at 75 Lake Drive in Hamworthy. During World War II, the Boat House was requisitioned and it was from here that the commanders of landing craft received their orders for the D-Day invasion.

The glass domes in the auction sold for varying prices – the one on Deck A went with the grand staircase for £1,850 (a huge sum in those days), while the dome from the tourist-class lounge was sold, along with 180 feet of teak panelling, for 130 guineas. In comparison, the dome from the tourist-class smoke room on Deck B was a snip at 42 guineas – about equivalent to the price of a Fat Face hoodie.

Address Fat Face, 71–73 Old Christchurch Road, BH1 1EW, +44 (0)1202 557231,
www.fatface.com/store/bournemouth/70217 | Getting there A 7-minute walk through
town from Bournemouth Square. The dome skylight is on the first floor of the shop. |
Hours Mon–Sat 9am–5.30pm, Sun 10.30am–4.30pm | Tip The original owner of the
Riviera Hotel in Alum Chine, Alex Callaghan, was a purser on the *Mauretania*, and also
worked on the *Queen Elizabeth* and *Queen Mary*. With the money he earned, he bought
the hotel, then named the function rooms after cruise liners within the Cunard fleet – the
Mauretania, Britannic and Caledonia Suites (www.rivierabournemouth.co.uk).

35 Donkey Trekking
Seek sanctuary in the woods

There are more than 40 million donkeys in the world. Two of them – Arthur and Ulysses – are ready to walk with you along tracks, through woods and around farmland near Fordingbridge. Leading one of them by a rope (while trying to stop them from grazing on the foliage), you'll be accompanied by their owner Marta Ferrari, an Italian equine vet who's travelled the world in the name of donkey welfare.

Having worked with the charity SPANA (Society for the Protection of Animals Abroad) and other small charities such as MAWO (Meru Animal Welfare Organization), Marta has visited countries including Tunisia, Morocco, Tanzania and Mauritania, where donkeys are the backbone of local communities, carrying water, carting goods to markets and doing farm work. Sadly, some areas are so poor that the donkeys are fed cardboard as there's no straw or hay. Even sadder, around 4.8 million donkeys are killed every year for their skin, which is used in the production of ejiao, a gelatine used in traditional Chinese medicine, food, drink and beauty products. One woman who Marta met in Tanzania had her donkey stolen as part of the donkey-skin trade, meaning she lost her trusty helper for daily chores, causing financial loss to her family.

Back in the New Forest, thankfully, Arthur and Ulysses are healthy, safe… and pampered. After their trek, you can give them a massage (brush) and Marta will give them a pedicure (clean their feet with a hoof pick). She's even bought them 'donkey trainers' to protect their hooves if needs be.

As you're brushing them, you'll notice they have a dark cross on their backs, as all donkeys do. Some believe this symbolises the crucifix, as a donkey carried Jesus to Jerusalem on Palm Sunday.

Marta began her Walk Beside Me treks in 2020 and hopes that her stubborn, curious and oh-so-cute sidekicks bring visitors as much joy as they bring her. *Hee-haw!*

Address Near Fordingbridge, +44 (0)7906 386334, www.donkey-trekking.com | Getting there Bus X3 to Fordingbridge Post Office, then a long walk or taxi ride, depending on where the trek is taking place | Hours Treks run year-round but are weather dependent | Tip Turn your day trip into a minibreak and stay at nearby West Park Farm (www.westparkfarm.co.uk). From here, explore the surrounding woodland, which is covered in bluebells during April and May.

36 The Ducking Stool
This is torture

Women, do you know your place? If you'd have been found guilty of brawling, verbal abuse or acting in an otherwise antisocial way in the 14th century, it would have been at the end of this ducking stool, suspended over a body of water. This punishment device would see the offender strapped to the wooden contraption, then dunked into the river as many times as their sentence dictated. Public humiliation was the order of the day, but many ducking-stool punishments led to death, the victim dying from shock or drowning. Contrary to popular belief, it's unlikely these rigs were used in Britain to identify witches – a different water-dunking technique was reserved for those suspected of witchcraft.

This ducking stool next to the River Avon in Christchurch is a replica, placed here in 1986, close to where its original position would have been. The silt in the river has accumulated over the years, so the water would have been much deeper when the original was in use. The gruesome nature of this apparatus is now at odds with the charming pink, blue and green pastel-coloured houses that line the surrounding Ducking Stool Walk. It's a very pleasant place for a stroll, torture implement aside.

Ducking stools have been depicted in a few films over the years, including the 1934 *Babes in Toyland*, where Laurel and Hardy (see ch. 27) are arrested for burglary and sentenced to be dunked in the ducking stool then banished to Bogeyland; and a type of ducking stool is seen in the 1975 *Monty Python and the Holy Grail*. More recently, a ducking stool appeared in Terry Pratchett and Neil Gaiman's *Good Omens* book but, unfortunately, was cut from the TV show (starring David Tennant, Michael Sheen and Jon Hamm) for health and safety reasons. Apparently, dunking children on screen is frowned upon, so the makeshift ducking stool was replaced with a much more palatable tyre swing.

Address Ducking Stool Lane, Christchurch BH23 1DS | Getting there Bus 1 or 1a to Priory Corner | Tip Other forms of public humiliation included time in a pillory, whipping through the market, being spun in a whirlygig, and exposure in the stocks. Not far from the ducking stool, in front of the ruins of Christchurch Castle, is Ye Olde Stocks, which you can put your arms through.

37 The Echo Building
Read all about it!

J. R. R. Tolkien… Robert Louis Stevenson… Mary Shelley (see ch. 61)… Bournemouth has many connections to famous writers. But they're not all six feet under; some are alive and kicking – and began their career at the *Bournemouth Echo*. From 1977 to 1979, American travel writer Bill Bryson was the local rag's sub-editor. His time there provided much inspiration for his 1995 best-selling *Notes from a Small Island*, and the 'sequel' *The Road to Little Dribbling*, published in 2015. He describes the *Echo* building as 'splendid' and 'vaguely Art Deco', but is less complimentary of his work space, 'borrowed from a Dickens novel', and his 'cadaverous' colleagues. Some well-known journalists also cut their teeth at the *Echo*, including Anne Diamond, Mark Austin and Pat Sloman.

One of Bournemouth's most iconic structures, the 1934 Grade II-listed building stands on the site of Richmond Villa, which was demolished – along with other dwellings on Albert Road and Yelverton Road – to make way for the Purbeck- and Bath-stone beast. Sporting more glass than any other building in town when first constructed, it was designed by architects A. J. Seal & Partners, who also created Palace Court Hotel on Westover Road (currently Premier Inn), Conning Towers at 75 Haven Road and the Regent Centre in Christchurch (see ch. 81). Now Seal Designs, the firm's logo is a nod to the detailed façade of the Echo building.

The printing presses were moved to Weymouth in 1997 and the room was later converted into the Print Room Brasserie and Ink Bar. Alas, they have since called time… which is what the huge clock on the building did until 2012. Up until then, the master clock controlled several slave clocks inside, to keep workers on the same time schedule.

Today, *Echo* staff still work here, but the four floors are also used by other companies in the tech, digital, media, advertising and creative industries. Bill Bryson is long gone, now counting his millions.

Address Richmond Hill, BH2 6HH, +44 (0)1202 554601, www.bournemouthecho.co.uk | Getting there A short walk from Bournemouth Square | Tip Walk around the corner to 2 Albert Road, which is where the *Echo* head office stood when the newspaper was founded in 1900. It's now ice cream parlour Creams, where you can 'get the scoop' of a totally different kind.

38 Egyptian Mummy
That's ancient history

If dead things interest you, you'll love the Bournemouth Natural Science Society museum. Home to around 350 stuffed birds and other animals (including the extinct passenger pigeon, which died out in 1914), thousands of butterflies and other insects, and all manner of weird and wonderful creatures preserved in formaldehyde in the Curiosity Cupboard, perhaps the most fascinating dead thing 'living here' is the ancient Egyptian mummy.

Dated back to around 700 B.C., the hieroglyphics on the coffin indicate that the occupant's name was Tahemaa. Originally from Thebes (modern Luxor), she found herself in Bournemouth via Salisbury Museum, which donated her in 1922. She arrived in the UK in 1820, perhaps via tomb raiders, who would often sell stolen artefacts to tourists as souvenirs.

In order to discover more about her past, Tahemaa was X-rayed in 1993 and 2009. The scans showed a bag between her knees containing her internal organs, which would have been removed during the mummification process. One organ that, unusually, wasn't removed was her brain. It was standard practice in ancient Egypt when preparing a body for the afterworld to remove the brain via a broken bone at the back of the nose. Curiously, Tahemaa's nasal bones remain intact.

Another exhibit in the Egyptology room is the cast of the Rosetta Stone. Only four casts of the stone were made in the world and it's believed this is one of them. The 196 B.C. original – which held the key to deciphering Egyptian hieroglyphs – resides in the British Museum in London, and is its most visited exhibit. The Egyptian obelisk at Kingston Lacy in Wimborne also played a part in the emergence of a hieroglyphic 'alphabet', with the cartouches (ovals with royal names written in) on the Rosetta Stone being compared with the ones on this obelisk. Without this, Tahemaa's name would have remained a mystery.

Address Bournemouth Natural Science Society, 39 Christchurch Road, BH1 3NS, +44 (0)1202 553525, www.bnss.org.uk | Getting there Bus 1, 1a or m2 to St Swithun's Roundabout. The mummy is on the first floor, in the Egyptology Room. | Hours Tue 10am–4pm. Check the website for details of open days, which run throughout the year | Tip As well as dead things, the museum is also full of really old things. Amongst the fossils, dinosaur footprints and teeth from an Ice Age woolly mammoth, you'll also find the wooden remains of a fossil forest dating from around 5,000 B.C., discovered near Bournemouth Pier in 1979.

39 Ejector Seat
Winging it

'I feel the need… the need for speed!' If you're a *Top Gun* fan, you may find yourself quoting this line, imagining a shirtless Tom Cruise playing volleyball, or Kelly McGillis 'taking your breath away' as you sit in this ejector seat at the Bournemouth Aviation Museum. This model is a Type 3H, produced by the Martin-Baker Aircraft Company, which is internationally renowned for its assisted aircraft escape systems. It has delivered more than 70,000 ejector seats to 93 air forces around the world, and there are currently over 17,000 seats in service in 54 different aircraft types. In the 70 years the company has been operating, its equipment has saved 7,633 lives.

Tragically, Red Arrows pilot Jon Egging was unable to use his ejector seat and lost his life when his aircraft crashed into a field near the Aviation Museum on 20 August, 2011. There is a model of his Hawk T1A plane as a tribute to him at the entrance to the museum. There's also a memorial on the East Cliff.

Ejector seats such as this are used in fighter jets like the SEPE-CAT Jaguar, Hawker Hunter, Gloster Meteor, Jet Provost T5 and English Electric Lightning, all of which are on display here. The museum has around 20 aircrafts – either in full or in part – including a Vickers Viscount, in which Yuri Gagarin, the Soviet Air Forces pilot and cosmonaut who was the first person in outer space, once sat in the cockpit. You can climb on-board The Queen's Flight, a British Aerospace 125 plane that *may* have transported Her Majesty herself, but has *definitely* had Margaret Thatcher, George Osborne and other senior government officials as passengers.

There's also the pint-sized Colomban Cri-Cri, the world's smallest twin-engined manned aircraft; and the CMC Leopard, of which only two were ever made. Bring your curiosity – you're able to climb into cockpits, press buttons, fiddle with levers and play with all manner of other doohickeys.

Address Bournemouth Aviation Museum, Merritown Lane, Christchurch BH23 6BA, +44 (0)1202 473141, www.bamhurn.org | Getting there Bus 737 Jetbus to Adventure Wonderland (the museum is opposite). The ejector seat is inside the main cabin with the RAF crest on the front. | Hours Daily (excluding Christmas Day and Boxing Day), summer 10am–5pm, winter 10am–4pm | Tip Look out for 'Saucy Sal', the provocative pin-up painted on the side of the Handley Page Victor bomber, an aircraft used as a tanker to refuel RAF aircraft in the Falklands War.

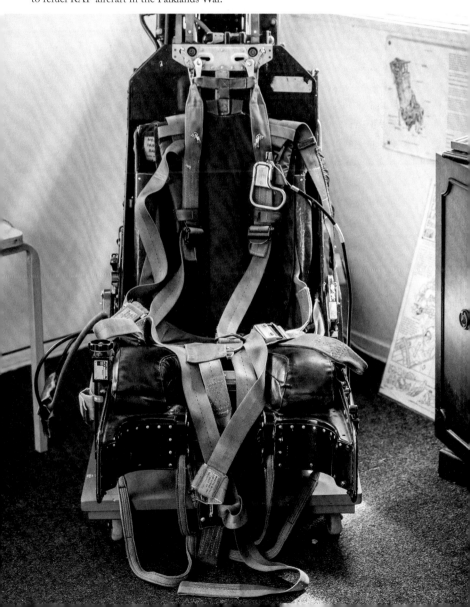

40 Elephant Mural
With a trumpety trump!

Let's talk about the elephant in the room. Or, more accurately, the six elephants on the wall.

Although these days you're far more likely to encounter a flock of pigeons on Boscombe's high street than a herd of elephants, this wasn't the case in the 1900s. You may also have seen lions, tigers, leopards, monkeys, polar bears, Himalayan bears, sea lions and even a boxing kangaroo. Back then, a number of travelling circuses – such as Billy Smart's, Chipperfield's, Bertram Mills and the Royal Italian Circus – visited the town to perform in the Hippodrome (now the O2 Academy Bournemouth).

Adopting a mammoth marketing strategy, the elephants would be paraded down the high street to drum up business. Nellie's friends could also be seen trundling down Sea Road towards the beach for a bathe and frolic in the sea. On one such outing, a baby elephant went AWOL, much to the public's dismay! In 1971, another wayward elephant was photographed entering The Bell Inn in Pokesdown, with the image published in the *Bournemouth Enquirer*.

While some locals remain unconvinced of its existence, there is supposedly a tunnel running underground from the O2 to Kings Park, said to have been used to transport some of the more fearsome animals to the theatre, so as not to alarm the public. Some of the cages used for the animals are apparently still in the basement of the O2.

Fast-forward to now and we have the majestic Baha, Bosca, Bashita, Beryl, Bodhi and Beafy (so named by the local community following an online poll) to remind us of these days of yore. The 95-foot-wide, 20-foot-high mural was commissioned by Bournemouth Emerging Arts Fringe (BEAF) and created by artist Krishna Malla, aka Tech Moon. He also painted the *Fly on the Wall* mural under the flyover in Bournemouth Central Gardens (see ch. 107). His impressive, larger-than-life artworks are certainly hard to forget.

Address 600 Christchurch Road, Boscombe BH1 4SX | Getting there Bus 1a to Palmerston Road. The mural is to the right of the entrance to the Sovereign Shopping Centre. | Tip At the end of the precinct, you'll see a giant Dachshund painted over two freight containers, also created by the talented Tech Moon.

41 Faces in the Garderobe
Monks behaving badly

Everybody likes privacy when they're on the loo. Luckily for the monks of Christchurch Priory, these faces weren't added to their garderobe, or outside toilet, until many years after the dissolution of the monastery in 1539. 'Outside toilet' is perhaps too generous a term – it was simply a building containing a plank of wood with holes in, suspended over the millstream.

To see another place where the monks would perch, head inside the Priory to the choir stalls, where you'll find 39 misericords, some dating from the 13th century. These small ledges on the underside of the hinged seats would offer support to the monks, who'd engage in long periods of standing worship. Known as 'nodding seats', the monks would often nod off while propped on them.

In the late 1530s, when King Henry VIII was disbanding monasteries, convents, friaries and priories, the prior of Christchurch, John Draper, wrote to the monarch, pleading with him to spare the Priory, declaring how God-fearing and moral the monks were. If he'd been around in the 1960s when the garderobe was excavated, he'd have had egg on his face when gambling dice and a lady's slipper were found! Was it a case of 'what happens in the garderobe stays in the garderobe'?

Henry VIII spared the Priory but the ancillary buildings got demolished, which is where these faces may have come from. It's been suggested that the Priory was saved due to blackmail. As a younger monk, John Draper lived at Hampton Court and may have heard the king making his 'forgive me Father for I have sinned' confessions. In Draper's letter, did he threaten to reveal the king's innermost secrets unless he left Christchurch Priory standing? We'll never know. What we do know, however, is that after King Henry VIII disestablished the monastery, Draper was given a large house and a sizeable pension, and the monks were given pensions, too. Good job they'd lost their gambling dice.

Address Christchurch Priory, Quay Road, Christchurch BH23 1BU | **Getting there** Bus 1 or 1a to Priory Corner, then a 5-minute walk. Go through the front gate of Christchurch Priory, walk around the left side of the building and you'll see the millstream. Walk about a minute and the garderobe is on the left. | **Tip** Continue walking around the grounds and you'll see the sculpture crafted by Jonathan Sells to commemorate the 900th anniversary of the building of Christchurch Priory. Note the foot kicking a monk, which signifies the dissolution of the monastery. (Jonathan also created the Tregonwell/Creeke statue – see ch. 103.)

42 Florence Nightingale's Grave

Humble pie

It's 20 August, 1910. An 84-year-old Crimean War veteran – who's lost an eye – stands in the rain next to this grave to pay his respects to the exceptional woman who looked after him at Scutari Hospital in Istanbul in 1854. Like so many soldiers, Private John Kneller felt hugely indebted to Florence Nightingale and, given she was the founder of modern nursing and a pioneer for the improvement of healthcare, perhaps we all should.

Although Florence requested that her body be used for medical research after her death, she was buried with her parents in the family plot, not far from Embley Park (now Embley School), where she grew up. Not wanting a fuss, it was her wish that the inscription said simply, *F. N.*, with the dates of her birth and death. During her low-key funeral, a grand memorial service took place at St Paul's Cathedral.

Every year, on the weekend closest to her birthday, 12 May (now International Nurses Day), a service takes place here, welcoming nurses from around the world keen to honour their humble heroine. The Florence Nightingale bench was placed in the churchyard in 2020 to commemorate the bicentenary of her birth.

To learn more about the woman who is said to have reduced the death rate in Scutari Hospital from 40 per cent to 2 per cent, the first female to be awarded an Order of Merit, and the lover of statistics who made pie charts more user-friendly, pop into the church to see the exhibition on 'Flo's Window'. You'll find artefacts and personal items bequeathed to the church, along with a copy of the front page of *The Daily Mirror* showing Private John Kneller saying his final goodbye to The Lady with the Lamp.

Since that day, thousands of others have visited her grave, proving that her light still shines bright and inspires many.

Devoted
to the memory of
our mother
FRANCES NIGHTINGALE,
wife of
WILLIAM EDWARD
NIGHTINGALE, ESQ.
DIED FEBY 1ST 1880.

GOD IS LOVE. I JOHN IV. IV.

BLESS THE LORD, O MY SOUL
AND FORGET NOT ALL HIS
BENEFITS.   PS. CIII. 2.

BY F. PARTHE VERNEY
AND
FLORENCE NIGHTINGALE.

WILLIAM ED.
NIGHTINGALE
OF EMBLEY, IN THIS COUNTY
AND
LEA HURST, DERBYSHIRE.
DIED JANY 5TH 1874,
IN HIS 80TH YEAR.

AND IN THE LIGHT SHALL
WE SEE LIGHT.   PS.XXXVI.9.

Address The Church of Saint Margaret of Antioch, Hackleys Lane, West Wellow SO51 6DR, www.stmargaretswellow.co.uk | Getting there About 4 miles from Romsey train station | Hours The churchyard is always open and the church is open during daylight hours | Tip While you're in the area, visit the Calling Window at Romsey Abbey (www.romseyabbey.org.uk). The stained-glass window depicts the moment Florence Nightingale was 'called' by God to a life of helping others.

43 Former Free Age Press
Found in translation

The Russian writer Leo Tolstoy – most noted for his epic *War and Peace* – is widely considered as one of the greatest authors of all time. And it was here, between 1900 and 1913, that approximately 424 million of his words were printed. Previously a waterworks, now a residential area called River Park, Free Age Press was set up by Tolstoy's literary agent, Count Vladimir Tchertkov, who'd been exiled from Russia after clashing with the authorities. Along with about 30 fellow émigrés, he established Free Age Press as a means of translating, printing and distributing Tolstoy's religious and ethical works that were banned in his homeland. They were sent to London, Paris, Geneva, Berlin… and even smuggled into Russia.

More than 60 editions of Tolstoy's essays, diary entries, letters and short stories were produced here, including 'Where Love Is, There God Is', 'The Slavery of Our Times', 'A Great Iniquity' and 'A Murderer's Remorse'. A radical newspaper was also published, which reached many suppressed peasants in Russia. Printed on very fine rice paper, it was folded into four and sent to the country as an ordinary letter. Sneaky.

Tchertkov and the rest of the 'Tolstoy colony' lived in the 20-bedroom Tuckton House (demolished in 1965) on Saxonbury Road. They existed by Tolstoyan principles of vegetarianism and teetotalism, and had few personal possessions. The house had a strongroom that stored Tolstoy's handwritten manuscripts. It was impenetrable, with 18-inch-thick concrete walls, lined with firebricks, and a steel grille door. In later years, when Tuckton House was used as a nursing home (and had a photo of Tolstoy in the entrance hall), workmen were called in to convert the strongroom into a bedroom. Work halted when, after a week, they'd only managed to cut a four-inch hole through one of the walls. The room was kept intact, the matron using it to store her best china.

Address The Old Waterworks, River Park, Iford Lane, BH6 5NF | Getting there Bus 1b to Seafield Road, then a 7-minute walk. Look for the tall chimney and blue plaque on the side of the building. | Tip Tchertkov's mother had been visiting Southbourne since the 1870s and bought the holiday home Slavanka ('house of peace') on Belle Vue Road. This was pulled down in 2006 and is now Sunrise Senior Living.

44 Fossilised Ammonite
Rock on

The bristlemouth is the most abundant creature in the ocean; around 64 million years ago, it was the ammonite. And here, by Highcliffe Beach, is a rather impressive fossilised one. Ammonites became extinct along with the dinosaurs and, since then, scientists have identified more than 10,000 species. They are related to other cephalopods like the octopus, cuttlefish, squid and nautilus.

Once you've marvelled at this huge chunk of prehistory, turn left (if you're looking at the sea) to hunt for fossils and shark's teeth along the beach. Get on your hands and knees and sift through the gatherings of shingle and, with a little patience, you're likely to find some of Jaws' friends' gnashers. It's incredible to think that you could be the first human in the history of the world to touch a particular tooth, which was inside a shark's mouth – chomping its prey – some 40 million years ago!

Another impressive ammonite nearby is located outside the information centre at the Steamer Point Nature Reserve. The two-foot relic was discovered on the beach between Christchurch and Highcliffe in 2007 when coast-protection engineers dumped the rock (originally intended to support the groynes on the beach) onto the sand and the large limestone boulder split in two, revealing the fossilised coiled-shelled creature.

You can walk through the 24-acre nature reserve to Highcliffe Castle (see ch. 53), stopping for a swing in a hammock along the way. The Bournemouth Natural Science Society museum (see ch. 38) also houses five large ammonites, all believed to have been discovered in Dorset.

When you've had your fill of collecting sharks' teeth, mosey on back past the ammonite and you'll come to a big rock with a plaque marking it as 'Bill's Bench'. It reads: *Bill Booth 16-3-44 to 12-4-98. Surfed it, loved it, respected it. Enjoy the sea as much as he did.* Be like Bill.

Address Highcliffe Beach, Highcliffe, Christchurch BH23 5DE | Getting there Bus 1a to Highcliffe Recreation Ground, then a 10-minute walk. The ammonite is on the beach path in front of Cliffhanger Restaurant. | Tip Near Highcliffe Beach is Chewton Bunny (the term 'bunny' means a narrow valley or wooded ravine and is sometimes used instead of 'chine'), which has Chewton Bridge within it. Built in 1900, it was the first bridge in the country to be made from concrete.

45 Fred Abberline's Home

Bloody good at his job

It's ironic that Inspector Frederick George Abberline – who worked for the Metropolitan Police for 29 years – became best known for a case he didn't solve. Despite infiltrating the Fenian Irish terrorist group and being key in the Cleveland Street Scandal (the homosexual brothel that almost brought the government to its knees… so to speak), it was his involvement with the Jack the Ripper case that put him in the history books – and this plaque on the wall.

Born in Blandford Forum, Abberline moved to London to join The Met, until he retired to Bournemouth in 1904, living at 4 Methuen Road. This house was later demolished so the Wessex Way could be constructed. The plaque is on Abberline's final home, which has now been converted into flats. It was unveiled on 29 September, 2001, which coincided with the Jack the Ripper conference held in Bournemouth, where famous prankster Jeremy Beadle was master of ceremonies.

Abberline is buried in Wimborne Road Cemetery, which is also the final resting place of some of Montague John Druitt's cousins. Druitt grew up in Wimborne and was a prime suspect in the Jack the Ripper case. Another suspect was George Chapman, a Polish serial killer known as the Borough Poisoner, whom Abberline believed was the culprit of the Whitechapel murders, too. Abberline also theorised that the murderer could have been a woman, and DNA testing undertaken in 2011 on a letter believed to have been sent by the killer confirms this is possible.

There have been many depictions of Abberline in television programmes and movies over the years, notably by Michael Caine in the 1988 series *Jack the Ripper* and Johnny Depp in the 2001 film *From Hell*. Much creative licence was used, however, with Depp's Abberline being a psychic opium addict with a penchant for drinking absinthe. In reality, Abberline was described as looking and sounding like a bank manager.

Address 195 Holdenhurst Road, Springbourne BH8 8DG | Getting there Bus m1 or 5a to Unisys, then an 8-minute walk, or bus 2 to Ophir Gardens | Tip Could you murder a pub lunch with a sea view? Head to the nearby Overcliff Pub inside The Suncliff Hotel (suncliff.oceana-collection.com), which is where the aforementioned Jack the Ripper convention was held.

BOROUGH OF BOURNEMOUTH

'ESTCOURT' - 195 HOLDENHURST ROAD
THE FINAL HOME OF
INSPECTOR
FREDERICK GEORGE ABBERLINE
1843 - 1929
DURING HIS 29 YEARS WITH THE
METROPOLITAN POLICE
ABBERLINE GAINED 84 COMMENDATIONS
AND AWARDS
AND BECAME WELL-KNOWN
FOR HIS WORK ON THE CASE OF
JACK-THE-RIPPER

PLAQUE UNVEILED SEPTEMBER 2001

46   Freddie Mills Memorial

Was this boxing legend 'hit'?

Freddie Mills, aka the Bournemouth Bombshell, aka Fearless Freddie, has been described as the David Beckham of his day. He took his sporting achievements – becoming the world light heavyweight boxing champion in 1948 – and punched his way to superstardom as Britain's first sporting celebrity. He became a national treasure, hosting BBC's *Six-Five Special* and appearing in a number of radio shows, TV series, stage performances and films, including *Carry On Constable* and *Carry On Regardless*. But, rather than being remembered for his lifetime achievements, it's perhaps his death – and the mystery surrounding it – that keeps his memory alive.

Born in Bournemouth, raised at 7 Terrace Road (his house has since been demolished), and educated at St Michael's School, the boxing star's life came to an abrupt end at the age of 46 when he was found dead in his car, in an alley outside his London nightclub on 24 July, 1965, having been shot through his right eye. A verdict of suicide was recorded but many factors point to him having been murdered. He consorted with gangsters like the Kray brothers and some believe he was killed as he owed the 'wrong people' money, and that corrupt police officers took bribes to bury the crime. But others think that Mills *did* kill himself, citing various theories. One of the more outlandish is that he was the serial killer 'Jack the Stripper' and was scared that his arrest was imminent.

This memorial was unveiled near the aviary in Bournemouth Lower Gardens in 1979, not far from the old Westover Ice Rink, which is where many of Freddie's early fights took place. Due to repeated vandalism, however, it was removed and kept in storage, until it found a new home in the Littledown Centre.

Next time you visit the leisure centre for a swim, gym session or, indeed, boxercise class, look at it and think about the scrappy local lad who sure could pack a punch.

Address Littledown Centre, Chaseside, BH7 7DX, +44 (0)1202 055500, www.bhliveactive.org.uk/centres/littledown-centre | Getting there Bus 2 to Littledown Centre or bus X3 to Bournemouth Hospital, then a 5-minute walk. The memorial is downstairs by the disabled lift. | Hours Mon–Fri 6am–10pm, Sat 7.30am–7pm, Sun 7.30am–8.30pm | Tip Next to the memorial is a plaque and replica boxing belt commemorating flyweight boxing champion Dai Dower, considered to be one of the most successful Welsh boxers of all time. He worked at Ringwood Grammar School, then at Bournemouth University as head of sport for 21 years, and was made an MBE in 1998.

47 Frieda's Tearoom
Crumbs!

Eating scones is a serious business. People in Cornwall and Devon have been debating the 'correct' way to spread the accompanying cream and jam since the 11th century, when a cream tea was first served in the UK. In April 2021, Sainsbury's apologised to unimpressed Cornish people threatening to boycott the scone aisle when the supermarket displayed an image of this baked good with jam on top of the cream (rather than cream on top of the jam) in their Truro bakery section. 'Blasphemy' it was called! And let's not even get started on the whole 'skon' or 'skoane' pronunciation debate.

Regardless of where you sit on the jam/cream dispute, if you want to enjoy a scone (as part of a three-tiered afternoon tea), homemade cake, doorstep sandwich, all-day hearty breakfast, boozy brunch (bottomless Prosecco, anyone?) or just a cuppa, head to Frieda's Tearoom. The cute bunting, eclectic vintage crockery, flowers in teapots, mini teacups hanging from lamp shades, shabby-chic Welsh dresser and 'I never met a cake that I didn't like' wall hanging combine to offer a welcoming 'Grandma's house' vibe.

Previously an unfulfilled chartered accountant, Iranian-born Frieda turned her baking/hosting hobby into a business in 2011. She thinks of her customers as 'guests who pay' and is proud to have converted this once-greasy spoon into a cosy tea room. Frieda had a brush with fame in 2020 with BBC One's *Call That Hard Work?*, when she, a stable manager and a fisherman all swapped jobs to see how they'd fare. Rushed off their feet preparing food, serving customers and getting afternoon tea ready for the Tea Bus (which is sadly out of commission until at least 2023), the stable manager and fisherman both agreed: 'Yes, I do call that hard work!'.

You know what else is hard work? Deciding if you're a cream-then-jam, or a jam-then-cream, scone-eater. Perhaps it's best to try both ways to see what you prefer. It's a tough job…

Address 7 Stafford Road, BH1 1JH, +44 (0)1202 291981, www.friedastearoom.co.uk | Getting there A 14-minute walk through town from Bournemouth Square; bus 1, 1a or 1b to Wootton Gardens | Hours Daily except Tue, 2 Mar–30 Sept 9am–5pm, 1 Oct–1 Mar 9am–4pm | Tip Time for (more) tea? Visit the quirky Steam Vintage Tea Rooms on Poole Hill (www.bournemouthtearooms.com).

48 The Fusee Building

Ticking over nicely

What time is it? It's the mid-1800s and this building is full of women working a 70-hour week, producing fusee chains to be used in clocks and pocket watches to ensure they'll, er, run like clockwork. It was fiddly work, requiring superb hand-eye coordination, excellent eyesight and the patience of a saint. The chains were so minuscule – only fourteen-hundredths of an inch thick – they could be threaded through the eye of a needle, and so slight that 5,000 of them weighed only about one and a half pounds. 'Fusee-chain maker' made it into Tony Robinson's 2004 TV series *Worst Jobs in History*.

The fusee chain industry was brought to Christchurch by Robert Harvey Cox around 1784, set up where Superdrug now stands on the High Street (a blue plaque commemorates this). He employed girls as young as nine (small hands, good eyesight) from Christchurch Workhouse, now the Red House Museum, and established the monopoly on chain production in Britain.

In 1845, William Hart got in on the action and opened this factory. Note the tall, narrow shape of the 74-foot-long by 18-foot-wide building and the large windows on either side, allowing for maximum natural light. This light would have aided the workers in their precise task but it wouldn't have been enough to save some from blindness. They enlisted the help of the spring water from Tutton's Well (see ch. 105), which was believed to have healing properties for eyes.

At the height of the industry, there were three fusee factories in town, which cranked out millions of chains; one industrious woman produced 150,000 chain links in one year. It also became a thriving cottage industry, with many workers toiling by their windows at home. By 1875, however, due to changes in watch design, fusee chains were no longer needed; the factories closed and the final chain was made in Christchurch in 1914.

The industry's time was up.

Address 20A Bargates, Christchurch BH23 1QL | **Getting there** Bus 1 to Bargates; less than half a mile from Christchurch train station. The building is through the white pillars into the courtyard. | **Tip** Take a 1-minute walk to Christchurch Recreation Ground, where you'll find the New Zealand Gardens, planted with trees and shrubs native to Christchurch on the South Island of New Zealand. The plaque states: *Presented… as living evidence of the good feeling and close contact maintained over many years with our twin town.*

49 Gas Street Lamps
Flaming lovely

The story goes that C. S. Lewis was inspired to include the famous lamppost in *The Lion, the Witch and the Wardrobe* while walking home in Malvern, Worcestershire one snowy night and spying a gas street lamp similar to this one. Incidentally, he was with literary pal J. R. R. Tolkien at the time, who lived in Poole between 1968 and 1971.

No, you haven't stumbled into Narnia. This gas lamp – as well as another 27 – line the roads of Throop and Holdenhurst villages, having not been updated for electrical ones like the others around Bournemouth. Made by the Ringwood and Pokesdown Foundries, and installed between 1902 and 1910, these cast-iron lampposts became Grade II-listed 'buildings' in 1994, so they won't be burning out anytime soon – if ever.

Note that they aren't evenly spaced; as Throop Road is so winding, they were placed in such a way that you can always see a light ahead of and behind you. Running on a clockwork timer – a Gunfire Time Switch – they get checked and wound weekly.

From Gunfire to gunpowder, locals recall their memories of gas lamps around town from long ago. One 'pyrotechnician' climbed up, opened the door and chucked a firework in, blowing the gas mantle to smithereens. Someone else used to clamber up to light their illicit cigarettes from the flame. Another changed the times on the clock so they became illuminated in the day. Pranksters!

Both Throop and Holdenhurst villages are conservation areas, yet are close to the bustle of urbanity. The abandoned flour mill (see ch. 100), straw ducks on the thatched roof of the local master thatcher, and 'toads crossing' road sign offer no clue they are only about a mile from Castlepoint Shopping Centre. You won't encounter an ice queen, talking lion or flute-playing faun, but venture inside these charming pockets of rural life and you'll feel like you've been transported to a different world.

Address Throop Road, BH8 0DQ and Holdenhurst Village Road, BH8 0EF | Getting there Bus 2 to Cowdrey Gardens, then about a 10-minute walk | Tip Another local Grade II-listed building is the 1804 Throop House. Originally built by Lord Malmesbury as a dower house, in 1959 it became the family home of the Fishers. The eldest son, Adrian Fisher, went on to become the world's leading maze designer (see ch. 1).

50 GIANT Gallery

Larger than life

Paula the Polar Bear – who symbolises climate change – has paraded all over the globe to capture the attention of parliament, Barack Obama, Helsinki locals, and countless others asking, 'Is that... a real polar bear?'. In August 2021, the Greenpeace nine-foot-long, two-person puppet captured the attention of visitors to the GIANT gallery in Bournemouth. Taking a break from her activism against companies such as Coca-Cola and Shell, Paula was part of the 'Why We Shout – the Art of Protest' exhibition that christened the 15,000-square-foot space, which is the UK's largest artist-led gallery outside of London.

GIANT was the brainchild of Bournemouth-born artist Stuart Semple, who also co-founded Voma.space (the world's first entirely virtual museum), created the 'world's pinkest pink' paint colour, and is learning how to unicycle.

The gallery welcomes new exhibitions in its main space every three months, and in its project space every six weeks. Its opening night saw hundreds of people snaking along the pavement outside, some waiting 45 minutes to get in.

Once inside, they were met with an array of thought-provoking exhibits, including a double life-size sculpture of a homeless man, a giant inflatable of 1960s cartoon character Underdog, a series of bronze-cast suicide vests holding art supplies instead of explosives, and a huge medicine cabinet, which challenged Damien Hirst's similar 2012 installation. Oh, and an original Banksy.

It's not just rotating exhibitions that GIANT runs – it also puts on educational programmes, Q&A sessions, film screenings, and events, such as 'We are the Light (at the End of the Tunnel)', which featured an electronic opera and aimed to offer inspiration to guests during a time of global transition due to the pandemic.

GIANT is a dynamic injection of culture into the town. What will it put on next? Watch this space.

Address Bobby's, Bournemouth Square, BH2 5LY, +44 (0)1202 080072, www.giant.space |
Getting there Enter through the main doors of Bobby's and head to the second floor. |
Hours Mon – Sat 11am – 6pm, Sun 11am – 4pm | Tip Stuart also owns The Pot Shop,
an imported noodle hangout near Bournemouth Triangle (www.potshop.store).

51 Gravity Mural

Houston, we have a painting

And the Oscar goes to… Bournemouth University! At the 2014 Academy Awards, space sci-fi blockbuster *Gravity* – starring Sandra Bullock and George Clooney – scooped the award for Best Visual Effects. During his speech, visual effects supervisor Tim Webber thanked 'the incredible team at Framestore'. Part of this team included around 50 graduates from Bournemouth University (BU) and Arts University Bournemouth (AUB), as well as BU lecturer Adam Redford, who worked on the Hollywood hit as a texture artist. Framestore is a London-based animation and visual-effects company, with a studio in the Enterprise Pavilion on the Bournemouth campus.

An astronaut is included in the *Bournemouth – A History of Shaping the Future* mural, created in 2016 by Paintshop Studio (see ch. 107). It also highlights local talent in the shape of footballer Tommy Elphick, breakdance crew Second to None, and Robert Louis Stevenson's characters Jekyll and Hyde.

Gravity is just one of the universities' award-winning triumphs. In 2021, BU graduate Andrew Lockley won his third Oscar for Best Visual Effects, for *Tenet*, having previously won for *Inception* and *Interstellar*. In 2020, graduates from BU's National Centre for Computer Animation (NCCA) worked on all five films nominated for an Oscar in the Best Visual Effects category: *Avengers: Endgame*, *The Irishman*, *Star Wars: The Rise of Skywalker*, *The Lion King* and *1917*. Other Oscar-winning movies 'effected' by alumni include *Jojo Rabbit*, *Avatar*, *The Jungle Book*, *Ex Machina*, *Blade Runner 2049*, *Spectre*, *Inside Out* and *Frozen*. The *Harry Potter* films and *The Hobbit* trilogy can also be added to the list.

Such is the extent of local achievements in the film industry that, a few days after the *Gravity* Oscar win, David Cameron praised Bournemouth University in the House of Commons during Prime Minister's Questions. Everyone was over the moon.

Address Lansdowne Lane, BH1 1AN | Getting there Bus m1, 1, 17 or X6 to Lansdowne |
Tip Robert Louis Stevenson lived at Skerryvore at 63 Alum Chine Road in Westbourne,
where he wrote *The Strange Case of Dr Jekyll and Mr Hyde* in 1885. A commemorative garden
for the author stands there today.

52 Grazing Goats
Kidding around

If, when strolling along the East Cliff, you hear a '*maaaaaa*' sound, don't accuse your companion of bleating on – it's likely you heard the cry of the Boer goats living on the cliffs. These cliffs support more than 300 species of plants, plus rare lizards, butterflies, insects and birds. Since discovering that the area was being overrun by invasive greenery such as holm oak, garden privet and Japanese knotweed, the council introduced a herd of goats in order to chomp away the problem. And chomp they do!

Since the first goats arrived in 2009, the herd has grown and, now, Phoebe, Alison, Amy, Ben, Jerry, Nana, Derek, Hamish, Macbeth and their other billy (and nanny) friends have been so successful at keeping the vegetation at bay that a breeding programme has begun, to add to the gang. In July 2020, Nana and Derek became proud parents to Tom, Dick and Harry. The triplets were moved to a farm to be reared before they were old enough to return to the cliffs. The Facebook page 'Bournemouth East Cliff Goats' was set up to share their progress. The group's 920 followers heard all about Nana's engorged milk, the vet visits, the playing and napping in the sun and, sadly, Dick's death a few weeks after he was born.

In November 2021, there were 20 goats on the East Cliff. The goal is to increase this number, meaning most of the nine pens, running from Alum Chine to Southbourne, will eventually have five or six hairy inhabitants.

Mark, the local goat owner, who has an agreement with the council to keep his 'pets' on the cliff, has his work cut out for him. But it'll be worth it. The British Feral goats on the cliff at Honeycombe Chine have done such a great job that grass cover increased from 2 per cent in 2012 to 62 per cent in 2018. The amount of native grassland habitat and the number of butterflies and lizards have also increased. Quite the thriving nanny state.

Address East Cliff, BH1 3DN | Getting there Bus 1a, 2 or 5 to Lansdowne, then an 8-minute walk. It may take a while to spot a goat – be patient! | Tip Looking for goats can be thirsty work. Quench yourself at the Goat & Tricycle pub near Bournemouth Triangle (www.goatandtricycle.co.uk).

53 Highcliffe Castle
Where the 'king of retail' resided

This grand clifftop mansion has had many owners and tenants, including Harry Selfridge, who rented it for £5,000 a year from 1916 to 1922 as his country retreat. Founder of London department store Selfridges, the American multi-millionaire became a celebrity, known as the 'showman of shopping'. With his lavish lifestyle of gambling, womanising and overspending, he'd often use Highcliffe Castle to entertain guests, playing high-stakes poker in the library with the likes of tea magnate Sir Thomas Lipton and, once, hosting a charity fête for 5,000 people.

Selfridge spent £25,000 – equivalent to about £1 million – on modern bathrooms, a modern kitchen and steam central heating. A hefty sum to pump into a rental property. At the height of his wealth, he bought Stanpit Marsh and Hengistbury Head, where he had plans drawn up to build 'the biggest castle in the world', with 250 rooms, a Gothic fortress, theatre and Versailles-style Hall of Mirrors. Ultimately, his extravagance meant he lost his £60-million fortune; his dream house never came to fruition and he eventually sold his land to Bournemouth Council.

The man who championed the phrase 'the customer is always right' died almost penniless at the age of 90 in 1947. He is buried just up the road from Highcliffe Castle at St Mark's Church, near his wife, mother and youngest daughter's ashes.

For two days in 2015, Highcliffe Castle was closed to the public to make way for the cast and crew of the period drama *Mr Selfridge*, who were filming scenes for season 4, episode 2. Greg Austin, who plays Harry's son Gordon, grew up locally, attending Bournemouth School (see ch. 20). Throughout the series, look closely and you might spot a painting of Highcliffe Castle in Selfridge's office. You might also be inspired to hop on a train to London to visit the nine-floor store that changed the way we shop for ever.

Address Rothesay Drive, Highcliffe BH23 4LE, +44 (0)1425 278807, www.highcliffecastle.co.uk | Getting there Just over a mile from Hinton Admiral train station | Hours Castle opening hours: Sun–Thu 10am–4pm; check website for castle grounds opening hours | Tip Another prominent figure to grace Highcliffe Castle was Australian soprano singer Dame Nellie Melba, who was the most famous singer of the late Victorian era and early 20th century. Melba toast and peach melba are both named after her. Head to The Oaks and enjoy a peach bellini in her honour (www.oakshighcliffe.com).

54 Hotel Celebrity

Lights… camera… action!

Have you ever dreamed of sleeping with George Clooney, Beyoncé or, er, Ken Dodd? Now's your chance!

With 59 rooms dedicated to various celebrities – mainly film stars and singers – you can wake up next to your favourite pin-up. You can also dine with Mae West, Bette Davis, Marilyn Monroe, Elizabeth Taylor and Marlene Dietrich in the Divaz Restaurant, where you'll learn some fun Tinseltown facts. Like that Bette Davis apparently coined the name Oscar for the Academy Awards as the statue's bottom resembled her husband's, Harmon Oscar Nelson Jr.

There are 440 celebrities pictured throughout the building – along corridors, in the Birdcage Lounge Bar, in the Hollywood Restaurant… there's even a scantily clad David Beckham in the ladies' loo. At the entrance to the hotel, near the life-size Spider-Man and Batman, you'll find a headshot of each celebrity with their location; visitors are encouraged to go star-spotting. Cameras at the ready!

In the downstairs lounge lives a homage to Sherlock Holmes, with a large array of collectibles. From magnifying glasses to microscopes, bayonets to binoculars – plus his trademark pipe (see ch. 90) – feast your eyes on this fictional sleuth's crime-solving tools.

On the second floor, you'll discover a display case dedicated to comedian Tony Hancock, who lived here as a child when it was Durlston Court Hotel. The memorabilia exhibited includes three typewriters, one of which was donated by Alan Simpson and Ray Galton, who wrote much of Hancock's material, as well as the sitcom *Steptoe and Son*. Hancock made his first professional appearance in 1940 at what is now Avon Social Club in Springbourne, where there's a plaque commemorating this.

Whether you stay the night, enjoy a meal, have a drink, or simply come to surround yourself with the rich and famous, Hotel Celebrity is ready to roll out the red carpet.

Address 47 Gervis Road, BH1 3DD, +44 (0)1202 316316, www.hotel-celebrity.com | Getting there Bus m1 or m2 to the top of Bath Hill | Tip Outside the hotel, notice the phone box. Once located near the East Cliff, celebrities staying nearby would often use it to make calls to their lovers that they didn't want the hotel telephone switchboard operators to listen in on (and sell what they heard to the newspapers). The phone box became known as the 'lovers' line'.

55 Isaac Gulliver Tree

He carved out a life of crime

There are 5,081 council dwellings in Bournemouth. But only one has a tree bedecked with Dorset's most notorious smuggler, Isaac Gulliver – sitting on stolen barrels of liquor – out front. The western redwood had died and was causing safety concerns, so the council brought it back to life by commissioning this artwork in 2019, to celebrate 100 years of the Addison Act (which made it a national responsibility for councils to provide affordable housing).

Gulliver, known as 'The Gentle Smuggler' as he never killed anyone, lived in Kinson between the early 1780s and 1816 at various times. He ran a huge operation, with his team working across Dorset, Hampshire, Wiltshire and on the Continent. To retrace local steps of the famous bootlegger (perhaps with a swag bag of silk, lace, tea and gin over your shoulder), pop into The Kinson Hub or Kingfisher Barn at Stour Valley Nature Reserve for a Gulliver's Trail map. Taking you on a seven-mile walking tour, you'll hit up highlights such as St Andrew's Church, where contraband was stashed (see ch. 93); Gulliver's Walk inside Cuckoo Woods, one of Bournemouth's oldest woods; a footpath inside Turbary Common Nature Reserve thought to be a smuggling route; and the site of Gulliver's Tunnel in Millhams Mead Nature Reserve (see ch. 62).

This tree stands where Kinson House and Holt Lodge once were. Gulliver and his wife lived in Kinson House in 1815, and Charles Bennett, the first British track and field Olympic champion (see ch. 25), lived in Holt Lodge in 1931. The land was requisitioned by the council in 1940, and the properties you see now were built in the early 1950s.

Probably the oldest council house in the country is at 11 Castle Street in Christchurch, with the 1235 deeds stating it was owned by the borough. The building is now Dirty Gertie's Gin Parlour – an establishment Gulliver would almost certainly have approved of.

Address 1543–1545 Wimborne Road, Kinson BH10 7BE | Getting there Bus 5a to The Kinson Hub | Tip To see the wildlife portrayed on the tree in the flesh – otters, fish, butterflies, dragonflies, herons – take a stroll through Stour Valley Nature Reserve (www.visitstourvalley.co.uk), where you'll also find Muscliff Arboretum containing trees from around the world. The trees above Gulliver represent the ones he planted along the coastline to aid navigation of his ships.

56 Jane Goodall's Tree
A champion for chimps

To say that Dr Jane Goodall, founder of The Jane Goodall Institute, Dame of the British Empire, and UN Messenger of Peace, is 'kind of a big deal' would be like saying that Mother Teresa was 'quite a nice lady'. Lauded for her early discoveries and research into the lives of wild chimpanzees at Gombe in Tanzania, Jane has written around 30 books, been the subject of more than 40 films (including the Emmy-winning *Jane*, Oscar-shortlisted *Jane's Journey* – which had its UK premiere at Bournemouth University – and the National Geographic film *The Hope*), won over 100 awards, and boasts 3.5 million-plus followers on social media. Not bad for an octogenarian.

Jane Goodall is, in fact, a *huge* deal. Yet most residents of Bournemouth (where she grew up and where she lives when she's not globetrotting for 300 days a year) have no idea who she is – let alone her global influence. When this tree was planted on 31 January, 2011, Jane said: 'It's the first tree I've planted in my hometown. It's very rare here that anybody except the *Daily Echo* even knows that I exist, although in America and other places it's very different'.

And different it is! The Jane Goodall Institute, set up in California in 1977 to promote conservation, now has 23 institutes around the world. Jane's Roots & Shoots education programme has empowered tens of thousands of young people in over 65 countries, including many groups in the UK.

In 2019, Jane was part of the 'Statues for Equality' art initiative, which saw 10 inspirational women (such as Oprah Winfrey, actress Cate Blanchett, singer Pink and astronaut Tracy Dyson) transformed into bronze statues and displayed in New York.

Jane is extremely passionate about conserving the planet and has vowed that her organisation will plant five million trees as part of the One Trillion Trees Initiative set up by the World Economic Forum. This oak in Bournemouth Gardens is an excellent start.

Address Bournemouth Central Gardens, Bourne Avenue, BH2 6DJ, www.janegoodall.org.uk | Getting there Enter the gardens by the Bournemouth War Memorial and walk to the other side of the stream. If you're facing the tree, the memorial is directly on your right. | Tip Jane has her own rose. The Jane Goodall Rose was created by 'rose author' Christian Hanak and the first 400 were planted in the rose garden of Val-de-Marne near Paris. Another was planted in Poole's Compton Acres (www.comptonacres.co.uk).

57 Joseph Cutler Tiles
The face of Bournemouth

Many revellers enjoy a night on the tiles along Old Christchurch Road. Joseph Cutler has been doing so since 1877, when he built a parade of six shops here and adorned them with tile panels emblazoned with his face. Known for self-promotion, this strip was called Joseph's Terrace, but the number of tiles has dwindled and the only ones now visible are those outside DNA nightclub. One has been chopped in half through Cutler's face; he's likely turning in his grave.

Joseph Cutler was described as one of the 'liveliest and most provocative personalities in the public life of the town', as well as 'Bournemouth's little dictator'. A driving force in much of the town's development, while ruffling feathers with his unorthodox views, he got things done. He built 'Muriel' (later Cheam House) on the corner of Upper Terrace Road and Exeter Road, which is where controversial artist Aubrey Beardsley lived (see ch. 12). He also constructed Joseph's Steps on the West Cliff (later converted into the Zig Zag); conveniently, they led to the bathing machines owned by Cutler himself. How enterprising!

Elected an Improvement Commissioner in 1881, not everything he did was self-serving, though. He fought for women's rights at Bournemouth Town Hall (see ch. 102), proposed cheap rail tickets for the working class, and paid those working for him above the average wage. He also suggested a fire brigade, where he volunteered as a firefighter for many years, plus was a sergeant for the Artillery Volunteers. He served as a councillor and alderman, and campaigned for Bournemouth to have municipal status.

Despite all this, Cutler's contemporaries weren't always complimentary. Rival developer Henry Joy described the portrait on these tiles as 'a good likeness, even capturing the crack in his head'. Given everything Cutler did for Bournemouth, though, surely he can be forgiven this vanity project.

Address 224–226 Old Christchurch Road, BH1 1PE | Getting there A 12-minute walk from Bournemouth Square | Tip A member of the Burial Board at Wimborne Road Cemetery, Cutler is responsible for the attractive monkey puzzle trees and golden hollies that line the main drive leading to the chapel. He's also buried here.

58 La Fosse's Cheeseboard

Exceedingly good cheese

Crumbly, hard, soft, pongy, oozey, creamy, spreadable, mild, mature, velvety, smoked, squeaky… The 1,800-plus cheeses of the world come in many forms. If you want to sample some absolute corkers, try the award-winning cheeseboard at La Fosse B&B and Restaurant in Cranborne. Having won the accolade of Dorset's Best Cheeseboard, Mark Hartstone, owner, chef and fromage connoisseur, is constantly changing his cheeses depending on what his local suppliers recommend. One such supplier is the Book & Bucket Cheese Company, which produces 11 artisan cheeses, each named after a famous literary figure, some with connections to Dorset, such as Hardy, Blyton, Wilde and Austen. Mark serves around 10 cheeses on each board (going from mild to strong), displaying them on slate from the Delabole Slate Quarry in Cornwall, which is the oldest working slate quarry in England, possibly the world.

Each of the six bedrooms at La Fosse is named after a local cheese, so every door dons a piece of this slate, too, with the name written on. Some of these cheeses, such as Old Sarum, Win Green and Gold Hill (a cheese named after the hill in Shaftesbury made famous by the 1973 Hovis 'boy on a bike' advert, directed by bigshot Ridley Scott) are no longer made, but Old Winchester, Dorset Blue and Stoney Cross are still going (and tasting) strong. Above each bed hangs a photo of the room's specific cheese, taken by Robert Golden, who worked on the Mr Kipling Cakes adverts – of 'exceedingly good' fame – in the 1980s.

Perhaps the cheeses no longer produced will stage a comeback, like the Dorset Blue Vinny did, the production of which stopped after World War II. It wasn't until the early 1980s that the cheese's 300-year-old recipe was revived. While most cheese recipes call for full-fat milk, the Dorset Blue Vinny uses skimmed, meaning it's crumbly rather than creamy. Pass the crackers.

Address La Fosse, London House, The Square, Cranborne BH21 5PR, +44 (0)1725 517604, www.la-fosse.com | Getting there By car, take Wessex Way, B3081, B3078 and Wimborne Street to The Square | Hours Check the website as opening hours vary | Tip Visit nearby Cranborne Manor Gardens, which are accessed through the Cranborne Garden Centre. If you're not 'cheesed out', stop for a cheese scone, macaroni cheese or a Brie and cranberry sandwich (www.cranbornegardencentre.co.uk).

59__The Library of Liquor
Read (and drink) the room

A is for Absinthe, B is for Brandy, C is for Cointreau… Z is for Żubrówka. Welcome to the A–Z of alcohol, also known as The Library of Liquor. A speakeasy-type bar above The Larder House restaurant, it describes itself as a 'chamber of taste and high spirits'. In the way of books, it's not much of a library, but does display a smattering of publications, including *Päntsdrunk: The Finnish Art of Drinking at Home. Alone. In Your Underwear.*

Also on display in the dimly lit, red-velvet-sofa, cigar-menu-on-request joint are an elephant teapot, Oriental parasol, teeth-baring stuffed fox, phrenology ceramic head, fish vase, pair of swimming goggles, peacock-feather wreath and George Michael mirror… 'Eclectic' doesn't quite cover it.

Opened in 2013, the bartenders and first regular, Gordon Fong, designated themselves a lockable leather suitcase each, engraved their names on the front, nailed them to the wall and used them to store alcohol they wanted to save for a special occasion. In one still sits a limited-edition bottle of Johnnie Walker Black Label The Director's Cut Blade Runner 2049. Another hidey-hole for 'moonshine' is under the floorboards, where a Talisker 10-year-old bottle of whisky resides. Prohibition, eat your heart out.

While the vibe is playful, there's one thing The Library of Liquor takes seriously: cocktails. Often dedicating a whole week to a certain alcohol (Rum Week, Sherry Week, Gin Week…), spirited concoctions are measured, mixed, muddled – and sometimes blowtorched – with gusto. One cocktail that holds a special place in the heart (and on the lips) of bar staff is the martini. Not only do they serve the cocktail at events like the Three Martini Lunch, they also keep a running tally on the mahogany bar (which came from a pub in Scotland) of how many they've consumed: 3,564 and counting. Clearly the Library's top libation.

Address The Larder House, 4 Southbourne Grove, BH6 3QZ, +44 (0)1202 424687, www.thelarderhouse.co.uk/library-of-liquor | **Getting there** Bus m2 to Fisherman's Walk | **Hours** Wed – Sat 6pm to late | **Tip** For a more Polynesian vibe, head upstairs to Ho'Okō Bar, a Tiki bar specialising in rum and fun.

60 Macpennys Woodland Walk

Family trees

Window shopping doesn't have to involve windows. Venture into this charming Woodland Walk and you'll be surrounded by hundreds of trees, plants, flowers, shrubs and bushes, there for your browsing pleasure. If they take your green-fingered fancy, many of the same species can be purchased in the nursery – along with around 3,000 others. Don't worry if you can't tell your azalea from your rhododendron; much of the foliage is labelled, with the name etched on MacPennys Long Life Plant Labels, which have been made on the premises since the 1960s, and sold around the world.

The woodland is one of 3,600 private gardens opened up to the public as part of the National Open Garden Scheme. There's no entrance fee but donations are encouraged, and given to charities such as Macmillan Cancer Support and Marie Curie.

Once a derelict sand and gravel pit, the Woodland Walk was bought in 1951 by Douglas Lowndes as an extension to the nursery. He built it up over the years with rare trees, woody and herbaceous plants, alpines, heathers and bright flowers. The nursery's whole plot has grown from its original five acres to 17.5 acres. Douglas and his wife Betty lived in a bungalow onsite, which overlooked this wooded wonderland. Douglas' memorial stone sits beside his dog's, a yellow Labrador named William, and Betty's is next to the *Daphne bholua* 'Jacqueline Postill' shrub planted in her memory. She lived to the age of 96.

Now run by Douglas and Betty's son Tim, and his wife Vivien, the nursery was originally bought by the Lowndeses in 1934 from a lady who grew drought-resistant plants and sold them in pots for a penny each – hence 'MacPennys'. Once you've wandered through the 'living catalogue' Wooded Walk – taking in the vibrant hues and lovely aromas – you're likely to be inspired to spend a pretty penny here yourself.

Address MacPennys, 154 Burley Road, Bransgore, Hampshire BH23 8DB, +44 (0)1425 672348, www.macpennys.co.uk | Getting there About 3 miles from Hinton Admiral train station. Follow the *NGS Gardens Open For Charity* sign to reach the Woodland Walk. | Hours Mon–Sat 9am–5pm, Sun 10am–5pm | Tip Don't leave without treating yourself to some cake and a cuppa from The Robin's Nest Vintage Tea Rooms. A sign inside states: *We don't serve fast food. We serve GOOD food, as fast as we can.*

61 Mary Shelley's Grave

Her husband is all heart

When a person steals someone's heart, it's usually meant metaphorically. Unless, of course, the heart belonged to poet Percy Bysshe Shelley, husband of novelist Mary Shelley. Having drowned at sea at the age of 29, Percy was being cremated on an Italian beach when his friend plucked his heart (which, medical experts later surmised, had become calcified so refused to burn) from the funeral pyre and, back in England, gave it to Mary.

She kept it in a silk purse for 30 years, until her death from a brain tumour in 1851, aged 53. The heart was found in her desk a year after she died, wrapped in the poem 'Adonais' written by Percy, and is now buried in a family tomb alongside Mary, their son Percy Florence Shelley, his wife Jane, Mary's mother (feminist author Mary Wollstonecraft) and her father (political author William Godwin). Romantic or plain creepy?

Mary Shelley was no stranger to creepy, not least because she lost her virginity to Percy on her mother's original grave. She also wrote the Gothic novel *Frankenstein* at the age of 19. Published in 1818, the monstrous story has never been out of print. Shelley was no stranger to tragedy either, with the death of three of her children – and husband – bringing her much grief. Her fourth child, Percy Florence, lived a long life, however, and is the reason that his mother, father's heart and grandparents ended up in Bournemouth.

Having bought Boscombe Lodge (now part of Shelley Manor Medical Centre on Beechwood Avenue), he had intended to turn it into a home for his mother but she died before she made the move from London. It was her wish to be buried with her parents, so Percy had their coffins exhumed and reinterred here. He also paid tribute to his parents with an impressive marble memorial inside Christchurch Priory. Depicting Mary cradling her husband's lifeless body, it really tugs at the heartstrings.

Address St Peter's Church, Hinton Road, BH1 2EE | Getting there A 5-minute walk from Bournemouth Square. The grave is on the right side of the church, about halfway up the steps on the right. | Tip The Mary Shelley pub over the road used to be J J Allen department store and, over the festive season of 1958, housed Durrell's Menagerie, a collection of animals owned by famous conservationist, naturalist, zookeeper, author and TV presenter Gerald Durrell.

62 Millhams Splash

No good deed goes unpunished

In 1907, Hitler was taking the entrance exam to the Academy of Fine Arts Vienna. In the same year, German Emperor (Kaiser) Wilhelm II was being rescued from this offshoot of the River Stour – then known as Kinson Splash and now Millhams Splash. Both men became responsible for the deaths of around 95 million people in the world wars.

The Kaiser is widely believed to have started World War I in 1914 due to his aggressive foreign policy. When Kinson locals Jesse Short and Bill Hicks saw his car stuck in the ford seven years prior, they pushed it to safety, and the passengers were prescribed whisky by Dr Lamb, whose grave is in Kinson Cemetery.

Kaiser Wilhelm II, Queen Victoria's first grandchild, had been staying at Highcliffe Castle (see ch. 53) for three weeks during this time as a 'rest cure'. He'd enjoyed many days out, including to Kingston Lacy and Hurn Court, where he planted a tree on each property. He also hosted tea parties for children at the castle, and attended services at St Mark's Church.

It was in Highcliffe Castle's library that he, unknowingly, set the wheels in motion for him to become publicly vilified. The conversations he had there, as well as those while strolling to Mudeford with his host, Major General Edward Montagu-Stuart-Wortley, later appeared in *The Daily Telegraph*, in which he stated that the English were 'mad, mad, mad as March hares' and talked of England being humiliated 'to the dust'. Other rude remarks – that didn't make the newspaper – involved Christchurch Priory's organ, which he called 'shabby'. 'When I am King of England, I will buy you a new organ,' he'd bragged.

Had Short and Hicks known their act of kindness was being offered to such a man, perhaps they would have left his car's wheels spinning fruitlessly in the muddy water. You know what they say: keep your friends close and your enemies… stuck in a ditch.

Address Millhams Mead Nature Reserve, Millhams Road, Kinson BH10 7LN | Getting there Bus 5 or 5a to The Kinson Hub, then a 5-minute walk | Tip Venture further into Millhams Mead Nature Reserve to discover its 200 kinds of flowering plants, 50 types of birds and 24 species of butterfly. The various riverside walks lead to Longham Bridge, Stour Valley Nature Reserve, Canford Magna, Dudsbury and, er, the tip.

63__ The Miraculous Beam
Leading a splinter group

Turning water into wine… Feeding the 5,000… Walking on water… Jesus performed many miracles throughout his life. If the workmen constructing Christchurch Priory are to be believed, there's one more to add: lengthening a wooden beam and fixing it in place.

Already perplexed by the building materials being shifted from St Catherine's Hill (see ch. 94) to the current site of the Priory, after work began in 1094, the builders were left scratching their heads further when a mysterious carpenter joined the team – but never stuck around for mealtimes or when wages were paid. One day, a beam was hoisted towards the roof but was too short, so had to be lowered back down. Such large timbers, cut from trees in the New Forest, were costly and in short supply, so the builders were worried about how to proceed. They needn't have fretted; when they returned the next day, the beam was in position, with length to spare. The clandestine chippy was never seen again, and people believed it had been Jesus Christ. As such, the building became known as Christ's Church of the burgh of Twynham. As the legend spread, the growing town was called Christchurch Twynham, then eventually Christchurch.

Having been removed from its position when the roof was raised at the end of the 13th century, the beam was displayed on the floor and became a focus of pilgrimage. However, when it was discovered that pieces were being continually chipped off and sold as souvenirs, it was reinstalled up high, out of reach.

Both the St Catherine's Hill story and the beam legend could be examples of 'medieval marketing'. Miraculous stories were often spouted to attract pilgrims… and their money. The British Museum houses The Tring Tiles, a collection of 14th-century ceramic tiles with apocryphal scenes, one of Jesus lengthening a beam that had been cut too short. A wooden performance that, apparently, was repeated again and again.

Address Christchurch Priory, Quay Road, Christchurch BH23 1BU, +44 (0)1202 485804, www.christchurchpriory.org | Getting there Bus 1 or 1a to Priory Corner, then a 5-minute walk. Go through the Priory's entrance and head down the church to the Lady Chapel; the beam is high up in the passage (ambulatory) between the Lady Chapel and Great Choir. Only the end of the beam is visible. | Hours Daily 9.30am – 5pm, although periodically closed for services, weddings and funerals | Tip The Priory has a second 'miraculous beam'. During a storm in 1990, a pinnacle fell through the roof and struck said beam, saving churchgoers from injury, or death. The item was retrieved via helicopter and reattached (slightly crookedly). A stained-glass window commemorating this event now sits in Cloister Way (the passage between the church and the café/gift shop), along with other episodes in the life of the Priory.

64 Moose Kitchen
Settle into a poutine

You know an Italian restaurant will serve pasta and a Japanese restaurant will serve sushi. But what about a Canadian one? Er, maple syrup and pancakes? Well, yes, but so much more besides! Canada's national dish, poutine – chips topped with cheese curds and gravy – is served with gusto here alongside other huge-portioned plates. Co-owner Kay Butler may even wear her 'You had me at poutine' T-shirt.

Many meals are inspired by chef Sara Goldsmith's childhood memories in Vancouver. The Roast Beef Dip is a nod to the shopping trips with her grandma, where they'd order this drip-down-the-chin dish. Family is clearly important, with photos of Sara's parents – who moved to Vancouver in the 1970s to open an English restaurant – displayed in the trophy cabinet, alongside Moose Kitchen's awards.

Life and business partners Sara and Kay opened Moose Kitchen in 2017 with no experience, little money and a premises in Charminster hidden behind a bus stop. Yet, within seven months, it had reached Tripadvisor's number-one spot of local places to eat. In 2021, it moved to its current location, the site of former eateries such as Swiss Restaurant, Seychelles Gastronomy and Miri's. It's double the size of their previous joint – perfect for all the moose paraphernalia they've been gifted over the years. You could dine beside the cute needle-felted moose, the hand-painted moose plate, the illuminated moose head or the drawing of a moose singing, 'Hoots mon! There's a moose loose aboot this hoose'.

Besides moose, the walls are decorated with rock-music collectibles, including dozens of album covers. Kay and Sara share a love of rock, with Kay having once been in a band called Gone Feral! Here, they've found their rhythm – a winning combination of come-hungry grub and a welcome so warm you feel like you're eating at a friend's place. Sound appealing? Then Moose Kitchen should become your maple staple.

Address 53 Bourne Avenue, BH2 6DW, +44 (0)1202 517700, www.moosekitchen.co.uk | Getting there A short walk from Bournemouth Square | Hours Check the website as opening hours vary | Tip Want to see how other local pancakes and maple syrup stack up? Head to Cafe Boscanova at 650 Christchurch Road, BH1 4BP (www.boscanova.com).

65 Mudeford Postbox
Pushing the envelope

Royal Mail has around 115,500 postboxes across the UK, in about 800 different styles. This fluted, Doric column one by Mudeford Quay, dating back to 1856, is the oldest one in the Bournemouth conurbation, and is believed to be the second oldest in Dorset. The oldest working postbox in the UK is at Barnes Cross, near Sherborne, in Dorset. Both boxes have a vertical posting slot with a hinged flap, designed for the smaller letters of the past. It was originally believed that this positioning of the slot would make it more difficult to steal from. In the 1960s, the Mudeford postbox was going to be replaced with a modern one, more suitable for larger letters, but local residents objected and the Victorian one remains.

Postboxes display a royal cypher, indicating the monarch at the time they were put in place. Curving around the top of this one, either side of a crown, are the letters 'VR', which stands for Victoria Regina. Regina is Latin for queen, signifying that Queen Victoria reigned when this postbox was installed.

Many businesses have manufactured postboxes over the years, including Andrew Handyside and Company. In 1879, it secured a contract to supply large quantities, and it continued to make all varieties of postbox into the early 20th century.

The iron founder also constructed bridges, piers, lampposts and fountains. One such fountain can be found next to the playground entrance at Alum Chine Beach. Built in the 1880s, the disused water fountain with two intertwined dolphins on top has seen better days; the water spout, cup holders and lamp are missing, as is part of one dolphin's tail, and exposure to the sea air and inclement weather means the iron has rusted.

If you're so inclined, perhaps you'd like to write to the council asking them to spruce it up. There's a postbox in Mudeford just waiting for your letter.

Address Mudeford Quay, Mudeford, Christchurch BH23 3NT | Getting there Bus 1a to Dennistoun Avenue, then a 20-minute walk. The postbox is at the exit of Mudeford Quay, next to the no-entry signs. | Tip Just up the road from the postbox is the multi-award-winning restaurant The Jetty (www.thejetty.co.uk). The food is delicious and the views across the harbour even better. It really is something to write home about.

66 The Mystery Tomb
There were 10 in the bed... maybe

We were not slayne but raysd, raysd not to life, but to be buried twice, by men of strife, what rest couldth living have, when dead had none, agree amongst you, heere we ten are one, Hen. Rogers died April 17 1641.

This curious epitaph is etched on the side of a chest tomb at Christchurch Priory, and has had historians scratching their heads for centuries. A few theories exist as to who is buried here.

One suggests there are 10 corpses ('we ten are one'). During the siege of Christchurch, the Parliamentarians – having captured the town in 1644 and being attacked by the Royalists – were running out of lead for their cannon and musket balls, so dug up lead coffins to create extra ammunition, then reburied the remains in the grave of Henry Rogers. How did these desperate grave robbers know where to find lead? In medieval England, wealthy and important people were buried in such coffins, and Henry Rogers had been mayor of Christchurch. Yet who were the other nine well-heeled dead people?

Another idea is that, during the Civil War, Oliver Cromwell ordered for 10 bodies of Royalists to be dug up from their graves and hung on the gates of the town, after which they were slung into one common grave. If this was the case, Cromwell certainly got his come-uppance years later when his own body was exhumed and subjected to a posthumous execution, with his severed head displayed on a pole outside Westminster Hall.

Or could it be that there's only one body buried here? Some believe Henry Rogers was convicted of smuggling and sentenced to death by being hung, drawn and quartered. His body was split into 10 – four quarters of the torso, two arms, two legs, head and internal organs – and he was originally buried in a 'potter's field' with other criminals. His family weren't happy about this so, in the dead of night, dug him up and reburied him here.

Alas, we'll never know which grave tale is true.

Address Christchurch Priory, Quay Road, Christchurch BH23 1BU | Getting there Bus 1 or 1a to Priory Corner, then a 5-minute walk. Go through the front gate of Christchurch Priory and walk towards the main door; on the right is a small set of steps, and the mystery tomb is the second chest tomb in from the steps. | Tip To the left of the Priory's north porch, you'll see an area of unconsecrated ground with no graves on. Many years ago, this strip of grass was used for archery practice; these days, it's the perfect spot for the Santa-and-reindeer display at Christmastime.

67 Napoléon's Wine Cooler
So much to 'pour' over

While French military leader Napoléon Bonaparte lived out his final days in exile in Longwood House on the island of Saint Helena in 1821, he refused to eat or drink anything other than a glass a day of South African dessert wine Vin de Constance. This tipple, along with his other favourites – Moët & Chandon Champagne and the wines of Chambertin – were likely stored in this ebonised wine cooler, which was gifted to the Russell-Cotes Art Gallery & Museum in 1944. Located in the Dining Room, it's joined by an octagonal walnut table also owned by the controversial wine lover.

Merton and Annie Russell-Cotes built this opulent seaside villa – originally called East Cliff Hall – in 1901, and they loved to collect items linked to the rich and famous. In the A–Z Room, you'll find a piece of Marie Antoinette's dress dating from before 1793 (under 'Q' for Queen); in the Moorish Alcove is a bronze and marble bust of Ira Aldridge, the first African-American actor in Europe to play Shakespeare's Othello; and the Irving Room pays homage to Victorian stage actor Sir Henry Irving.

This renowned actor's signature appears in the visitors' book in the Main Hall, as do those of actress Ellen Terry, Prince Albert of Belgium and writer Oscar Wilde. Ellen Terry is said to have used the downstairs toilet (stencilled with pine cones in recognition of the town's famous pine trees – see ch. 75), as is Jeremy Paxman while filming an episode of *The Victorians* in 2009.

The Russell-Cotes travelled widely and brought home curios from all over the globe. In 1885, they spent seven weeks in Japan and acquired more than 100 cases of souvenirs and artefacts, many of which are displayed in The Mikado's Room.

Once you've explored, head to the café terrace, which has expansive sea views. No wine is served (sorry, Napoléon) but you can get cake. Which surely would have thrilled Marie Antoinette.

Address Russell-Cotes Art Gallery & Museum, East Cliff Promenade, BH1 3AA, +44 (0)1202 128000, www.russellcotes.com | **Getting there** A 10-minute walk from Bournemouth Square | **Hours** Tue–Sun 10am–5pm | **Tip** In 1876, Merton and Annie bought The Bath Hotel on Bath Road. Then, having discovered that the Prince of Wales (later King Edward VII) had once visited, they reopened it in 1880 as The Royal Bath Hotel.

68 NHS Grotesque
Carve for carers

During the start of the COVID-19 pandemic, did you stand on your doorstep and clap your appreciation for the NHS? Sculptor Rory Young did one better. As part of Christchurch Priory's £480,000 restoration project started in 2020, he crafted this 22-inch by 17.5-inch masked-medic grotesque out of Lépine limestone from France. Inspired by a photo of architect Columba Cook's niece – a doctor working in the intensive care unit – it took Rory and a colleague about four weeks to carve. He first created a full-scale polystyrene model of the head, which he plans to sell.

Five other grotesques and gargoyles that had become unrecognisable due to centuries of erosion have also been replaced with new offerings (a grotesque is a decorative stone carving, whereas a gargoyle acts as a spout to drain water away from the building). They include the former Christchurch mayor and burgess James Druitt; the Royal cypher in recognition of Queen Elizabeth II being the longest reigning English monarch; and a bespectacled Sir Donald Bailey, who developed the Bailey bridge during World War II (see ch. 13).

Another local building that has been adorned with new faces carved out of stone is Highcliffe Castle (see ch. 53). When the East Tower above the shop was rebuilt in 1998, two new grotesques were created: one of principal architect Jane Chamberlain and one of foreman John Hammer.

Rory created 10 other grotesques and gargoyles on the Priory, including a mermaid, bat, ram and deer. On the tower, there's a monk playing a psaltery, a winged St Matthew holding the Bible engraved with 'LIB GEN' to indicate the first two words of his gospel, 'Liber Generationes', and Bishop Ranulf Flambard, who founded the Priory. He's holding a money bag as he was imprisoned in the Tower of London for embezzlement. He was regarded by many as ruthless and selfish, the exact opposite of his most recent key-worker companion.

Address Christchurch Priory, Quay Road, Christchurch BH23 1BU | **Getting there** Bus 1 or 1a to Priory Corner, then a 5-minute walk. From the front of the Priory, take the left path and walk to the wall overlooking the stream. Look up and you'll see the NHS grotesque on the far right-hand side of the building. | **Tip** As well as being memorialised on the outside of the building, a plaque honouring Sir Donald Bailey can also be found inside, on the first pillar in the South Aisle. Placed here in the 1970s, it's the last plaque to have been added to the church.

69 Norwegian Wood Cafe
Baked beans and Beatlemania

'This bird has flown, So I lit a fire, Isn't it good Norwegian wood.' These are lyrics from The Beatles' 1965 song 'Norwegian Wood (This Bird Has Flown)', which snake across a wall inside Norwegian Wood Cafe, Bournemouth's first coffee lounge. Opened in the 1960s, this no-fuss eatery wasn't adorned with Beatles memorabilia until many years later, when local artist and mega-fan Jan Stone gifted some of his drawings and paintings of the Fab Four to the place.

This collection has been added to and now diners tuck into their baguettes, jacket potatoes, omelettes, beans on toast and all-day breakfasts surrounded by Beatles photos, gig posters, magazine covers and a plethora of framed records and album covers. Notice in particular the cover of *With the Beatles*, with the iconic shot of the lads' half-shadowed faces. This image was taken by photographer Robert Freeman at the Palace Court Hotel on Westover Road (now Premier Inn) in August 1963. George Harrison wrote 'Don't Bother Me' while stuck in his room feeling poorly at the same hotel. 'Norwegian Wood' was inspired by an extramarital affair John Lennon had been having, and it was alleged that the woman he'd been seeing was Sonny Drane, Freeman's wife. Lennon and his first wife Cynthia celebrated their one-year wedding anniversary in Bournemouth.

Between August 1963 and October 1964, The Beatles played more concerts in Bournemouth than at any other place in the world apart from London, Liverpool and Hamburg – 18 gigs in total, at the Gaumont Cinema on Westover Road (which became The Odeon and is soon to be flats) and the Winter Gardens (now demolished). The first appearance of The Beatles on American TV was filmed at the Winter Gardens by CBS. Police would patrol as hordes of excited teenage girls gathered in The Pavilion car park, hoping to catch a glimpse of the mop-topped dreamboats.

Yeah, yeah, yeah!

Address 1a Glen Fern Road, BH1 2NA, +44 (0)1202 293185, www.facebook.com/ norwegianwoodcafe | **Getting there** A 6-minute walk from Bournemouth Square | **Hours** Tue – Sat 9am – 4pm, Sun 10am – 4pm | **Tip** John Lennon bought a house for his Aunt Mimi at 126 Panorama Road in Sandbanks. It has since been demolished and the house built in its place is called 'Imagine'.

70 Old Pier Theatre

Anything to declare?

Do you have a British passport issued between 2015 and 2020? If so, flick to pages 20 and 21 and you'll find Bournemouth-born architect Elisabeth Scott with two of the buildings she designed – the Royal Shakespeare Theatre in Stratford-upon-Avon and the Pier Theatre on Bournemouth Pier. Elisabeth designed the Pier Theatre to look like an ocean liner, and the building hosted many comedy shows (*'Allo, 'Allo!*, *Last of the Summer Wine*, *Hi-de-Hi!*) and famous faces (Rod Hull, Bob Monkhouse, Sid James) between 1960 and 2013. It was converted into an activity centre with climbing walls and the world's first pier-to-shore zipline in 2014, and the outside sign was changed from 'Pier Theatre' to 'RockReef'.

Although Elisabeth wasn't an 'outspoken' feminist, she certainly did her bit for gender equality. In 1919, at the age of 21, she became one of the first women to study at London's Architectural Association. When she won the international competition to rebuild the burned-down Shakespeare Memorial Theatre in 1927, she employed as many women as possible to assist in bringing her design to completion. Elisabeth loathed being described as a 'female architect', rather than simply an 'architect', and was an active member of Soroptimist International Bournemouth, which works to improve the lives of women and girls.

It's ironic that, nearly 50 years after her death, her appearance in the 'Creative United Kingdom' passport would probably have riled her as much as it did today's feminists. When the passport – which celebrates Britain's art, innovation, performance and architecture – was introduced, outrage ensued as there are only two females portrayed (mathematician Ada Lovelace being the other), compared with seven men. Perhaps Elisabeth would have encouraged those who designed the passport to take a long walk off a short pier. Preferably one with an old theatre at the end.

Address Bournemouth Pier, BH2 5AA, +44 (0)1202 983983, www.rockreef.co.uk | Getting there A 10-minute walk through the Lower Gardens from Bournemouth Square | Hours Old Pier Theatre viewable from the outside. RockReef: Wed (adults only) 6–9pm, Thu & Fri 4–7pm, Sat & Sun 10am–5.30pm; PierZip Sat & Sun 11am–3pm | Tip Take a stroll along Bournemouth Pier and reflect on the fact that the world's first ever water polo match took place off of it on 13 July, 1876.

71 The Old Station Holmsley Tea Rooms

From choo choo to chew-chew

Do you like your sandwiches and scones with a side of history? In the days of yore, this place would've been alive with engines chugging, steam wafting and guards shouting, 'All aboard!'. These days, it's bustling with bike riders, ramblers and waitstaff calling, 'Table 21!'.

Originally opened in 1847 as Christchurch Road station as part of the Southampton and Dorchester railway, its name was changed to Holmsley in 1862. The station closed in 1964 following the infamous Beeching cuts (which you can read about inside the tea room in a framed newspaper article, with the headline 'Beechingisation!'). You can also order yourself some Wheel Tappers, an Inspector's Rarebit or a Porter's Lunch Box, then tuck in while admiring your train-themed surroundings of leather suitcases piled high, old timetables, railway maps and retro adverts encouraging you to 'Take Your Dog With You By Rail'. Venture into the garden and you'll find reminders of the tea rooms' past life in the shape of a semaphore signal, a *Crossing No Gates* sign and a white marker with '97' on, indicating that the location is 97 miles from London Waterloo.

In the late 1800s, Queen Victoria's son, Edward, would often disembark at Holmsley station with his mistress, actress and socialite Lillie Langtry, *en route* to their property in Bournemouth. In 1907, German Emperor Wilhelm II (see ch. 62) arrived at Holmsley to attend a conference at Highcliffe Castle (see ch. 53). Holmsley station was also the inspiration behind the fictional station 'Browndean' in the 1889 black comedy novel *The Wrong Box*, written by local resident Robert Louis Stevenson (most famous for *The Strange Case of Dr Jekyll and Mr Hyde*).

Holmsley Tea Rooms is the perfect spot for a slice of cake. And a slice of nostalgia while you're at it.

Address Station Road, Holmsley, Burley BH24 4HY, +44 (0)1425 402468, www.stationhouseholmsley.com | **Getting there** About 4 miles from Sway train station | **Hours** Daily Apr–Oct 10am–5pm, Nov–Mar 10am–4pm | **Tip** The railway was promoted by local solicitor Charles Castleman. 'Castleman's Corkscrew' (so-named due to its winding route) was the first railway line to pass through the New Forest. This route now forms part of the wider Castleman Trailway, a 16.5-mile track popular with walkers, cyclists and horse riders.

72 — Orchard Street

The one and only

Bournemouth has an array of Roads, Avenues, Places, Closes, Drives – even a Triangle and a Square. Yet it only has one Street: Orchard Street. When the town was being planned back in Victorian times, the powers that be weren't keen on the word 'street', thinking its working-class connotations were too lowbrow for their fancy new town. However, Orchard Street was already established, so it remained.

Lewis Tregonwell (see ch. 103), who founded Bournemouth in 1810, legislated against streets with rows of terrace houses to prevent the town from looking too 'industrial', preferring detached houses for a more sophisticated vibe.

This cul-de-sac is anything but fancy. The road – sorry, street – has one block of flats in Edmondsham House and serves as a shortcut into the town centre. The lane at the bottom leads to the high street (although, of course, it's not called Bournemouth High Street – it's Commercial Road). Back in the days of Tregonwell, there was an orchard behind Commercial Road, which remained until at least 1851. These days, the closest thing you'll come to an orchard is Andre's Apple Repairs shop on nearby Poole Hill.

This isn't the only local orchard to have vanished. Since the 13th century, ciders, jams and apple cakes have been produced from orchards all around Dorset but, over the years, their number has dwindled. The Purbeck Cider Company thought this was a crying shame so, in 2017, launched its Forgotten Orchard range.

It also has the Purbeck Characters range, with ciders such as the mulled Posh Spice; the medium-sweet Katy & Perry, made with Katy apples and Perry pears; the fruity Vix on the Beach, a tribute to the vixens roaming the Purbeck Hills; and the bittersweet Purbeck Pirate, named after a sheep who lost an eye to a murder of crows. If you like your tipple with barrels of personality, these will be right up your street.

Address Orchard Street, BH2 5LY | **Getting there** A 5-minute walk from Bournemouth Square | **Tip** There may only be one Street in Bournemouth, but there are plenty of Orchards – Orchard Gardens, Orchard Mews, Orchard Close and Orchard Grove. There's also Orchard Avenue and Orchard Plaza in Poole.

73 Pause Cat Cafe
Feline it

If you're a dog person, you may want to swerve this kitty hangout, home to 11 purring, meowing, snoozing felines – all with very different personalities, and very different backgrounds.

Michelle – a pure white puss – was found with her three kittens in a bush in Leeds in 2017, before being rehomed here. Tabby Petrus was raised with dogs, so likes to lick people and wag his tail when he's happy (most cats swish their tail when they're annoyed). All of the Pause residents have been rescued and all are now like the cats who got the cream in their forever café-home, run by staff who love them to bits.

Such is their devotion for their furry friends that they're happy to take the night shift. The cats are attended to 24/7, and many of them crawl onto the bed with whoever is sleeping over. Apparently, Maine coon Marijke and her fluffy fur take up half the bed.

Having stumbled across a cat café in Milan, owner Jaya Da Costa knew she had to bring the concept to Bournemouth. On 17 February, 2017 – World Cat Day – she opened her doors to the south's first cat café, and locals opened their hearts to her motley crew of moggies. One customer has visited almost 200 times.

As well as sipping a Meow-jito juice, Pussy Galore smoothie or Es-purr-esso coffee, visitors can attend events here, such as Cat Yoga or Pampurr, where they get a massage and their claws (nails) done. Or they may choose to flick through one of the books on display, like *How to Tell if Your Cat is Plotting to Kill You* or *Crafting With Cat Hair*.

Spread over two floors, the café gives the cats plenty of space to roam, with scratching posts, suspended bridges, cubby holes, fake mice and other toys to toss about and, of course, customers to lavish them with love and affection. Had they not been taken in by Jaya and her team, their nine lives may have run out. Well, they do say that cats always land on their feet.

Address 119 Old Christchurch Road, BH1 1EP, +44 (0)1202 240194, www.pausecatcafe.co.uk | Getting there A 5-minute walk from Bournemouth Square | Hours Check the website as opening hours vary | Tip A few doors down is restaurant Kala Thai (www.kala-thai.com). Many Buddhist temples in Thailand act as 'cat refuges', where monks take strays in, then feed and care for them. Much like Jaya has done.

74 Picnic Park Deli

Sandwiched between the trees

Today Bournemouth, tomorrow Nashville! This was certainly the case for young country singer Nia Nicholls who, having performed amongst the trees and squirrels at Picnic Park Deli, went on to record her tunes in Music City itself. Nia's songs have been played on BBC radio and her single 'Jessica' was recorded with artists who have played with Faith Hill, Taylor Swift and Tim McGraw. Nia is just one of the many singers to have performed at open-air café Picnic Park Deli since it opened in 2016.

Set up by friends Adam and Marta, their goal was to create a relaxed social space where visitors can unwind, recharge and tuck into a delicious posh cheese melt. Or play a game of ping-pong if the mood strikes. More than just a café, as well as the live music the venue hosts, it also puts on salsa dancing, Bollywood dancing, box-ercise training, HIIT workouts, wellbeing sessions, arts and crafts classes, meditations, 'Dancing Through the Decades' lessons, chess matches and silent yoga (see ch. 89).

Situated next to the Pavilion Theatre, Picnic Park Deli has become a regular lunch spot for celebs performing there, including singer and TV presenter Jane McDonald, ex-*EastEnder* Rita Simons and the stars of *Strictly Come Dancing*, as well as AFC Bournemouth footballer David Brooks.

The terrace, complete with huge cushions, deckchairs and a lounging deck, overlooks Bournemouth Lower Gardens with the Big Wheel as a focal point. The aforementioned posh cheese melts are part of the casual yet cool menu – think halloumi sticks with chilli jam, smashed avocado on sourdough, and salted-caramel iced lattes. The melts are named after local figures – The Proud Mary after Mary Shelley (see ch. 61), The Sir Merton after Sir Merton Russell-Cotes (see ch. 67) and The Mini Plain Jane after Jane Goodall (see ch. 56). Who knows, if she hits the big time, maybe one day there will be a Nia Nicholls?

Address Westover Gardens, Westover Road, BH1 2BY, +44 (0)7825 394183, www.picnicparkdeli.com | **Getting there** A 5-minute walk from Bournemouth Square | **Hours** Daily 10am–6pm | **Tip** Next to Picnic Park Deli is the 50-year-old Bournemouth Aviary, which houses a huge array of birds, including the chatty yellow-crowned parrot. He's very sociable and may try to engage you in conversation with: 'Hello', 'Are you local?' and 'Nice cup of tea'.

75 Pine Walk

A breath of fresh air

'Bournemouth: The Centre of Health and Pleasure.' This was the headline on an advertising poster for the town in the 19th century. A more recent poster, made by cheeky artist Jack Hurley, reads: 'Bournemouth: The Penultimate Destination'.

Indeed, Bournemouth wasn't known for years as 'God's waiting room' for nothing. In the mid-1800s, the town was marketed as an upmarket health resort to visit if you were ill. The health-giving properties and scent of the local pine trees would cure respiratory ailments such as tuberculosis… apparently. Queen Victoria's physician praised the value of pines, declaring they were 'among Bournemouth's best doctors'. Such was the widespread belief in pine trees' remedial powers, the Pines Express train would carry convalescents and hypochondriacs alike from Manchester to Bournemouth daily between 1927 and 1967. Even author Robert Louis Stevenson and artist Aubrey Beardsley (see ch. 12) moved here in a bid to get some colour back in their cheeks.

It's been estimated that around three million pine trees had been planted in Bournemouth by 1890 – a combination of Scots, Monterey, Corsican, Austrian, Crimean and maritime (also known as Bournemouth) pines – by land owners such as Sir George Ivison Tapps and the Talbot sisters (see ch. 97). The three main woods were Talbot Woods, Branksome Woods and Westover Gardens. Now, primarily due to urbanisation, fewer than 100,000 pines remain.

A significant cluster still standing is at Pine Walk. Until 1917, this attractive tree-lined promenade was called Invalid's Walk, a nod to the raspy-breathed visitors being pushed along in their bath chairs. Today, it's shrugged off its reputation as a boulevard for the old, sick and dying – and while the trees may not do much for your physical health, take a stroll through this towering 'paradise of pines' and your mental health will likely enjoy a boost.

Address Lower Gardens, BH1 2BY | **Getting there** A short walk through the gardens from Bournemouth Square. Pine Walk is the path directly behind the bandstand. | **Tip** Stroll to the Bournemouth International Centre (BIC) to see the town's coat of arms, complete with Latin motto *Pulchritudo et Salubritas* (beauty and health) and pine tree sprouting out the top.

76 Poole Hill Brewery
On the hop

Around 300 species of birds live in Bournemouth. Jennifer Tingay, owner and head brewer at Poole Hill Brewery, chose eight of these to adorn the bottles of her Southbourne Ales. There's a skylark (which breeds at Hengistbury Head) on the Headlander Bitter; a kestrel (which hovers near Fisherman's Walk Cliff Lift) on the Cliff Riser Pale Ale; and a cormorant (which suns itself on groynes on Southbourne Beach) on the Sunbather Red Ale. The collective name for a group of cormorants is a 'gulp' – how very apt! These labels – drawn in a similar style to 1930s travel posters – scooped the Label of the Year accolade in 2015.

Set up in 2013, Southbourne Ales and Poole Hill Brewery have won many other awards, including three at the 2021 London Beer Competition. Jennifer appeared on the front page of *The Daily Telegraph*'s Business section on 22 June, 2020, with a photo of her sifting hops. The caption read: 'Hops and dreams'.

A variety of hops and malts are used in the beers, depending on the flavour that's required. During the brewery tour, they are passed around for a smell, and visitors are taken through the brewing process, being shown machines like a mash tun, wort kettle and fermentation vessel. The guide explains that the by-product is given to a farmer in Throop to feed his cattle: 'Apart from the staff, nothing gets wasted'. Some of the larger breweries send their by-product to Marmite.

Besides the 20-barrel brewery, there's a taproom where the fruits of Jennifer's labour can be enjoyed. Decor includes a wall bedecked with guitars, violins, accordions, a banjo and a bongo. Live music gets visitors' toes tapping most evenings and Sunday afternoons. A new brand of beer – Tingay's – has been introduced and there's talk of whisky being distilled here, too. Just like for the birds on the labels, it seems the sky's the limit.

Address 41–43 Poole Hill, BH2 5PW, +44 (0)1202 557583, www.poolehillbrewery.com | Getting there A 10-minute walk from Bournemouth Square | Hours Wed–Sat 3–11pm, Sun 3–10pm | Tip If all those brews make you hungry, head down the hill to Ojo Rojo (www.ojo-rojo.co.uk), a restaurant and bar specialising in Mexican tapas food.

77_The Potting Shed
Blooming delicious

Fish-finger sandwiches… Welsh rarebit… Rhubarb and apple crumble… At The Potting Shed, comfort food is the order of the day. Self-proclaimed 'feeders', owners Lee and Lydia offer customers a hug on a plate and, as well as serving traditional home cooking (including Sophie's Sandwich, a sausage sarnie named after a waitress who refuses to eat anything else), they also add flair with dishes like roasted squash with Mediterranean rice, mozzarella and basil; beetroot, mushroom and cashew burgers; and spaghetti baguettes (pure carb-on-carb heaven). The menu is seasonal, so is updated regularly with fresh ingredients, many of which – including edible flowers calendula, viola and lavender – are grown in 'Mr McGregor's Garden', signposted with the warning: *No rabbits!*

What isn't grown in the garden is sourced locally, such as the meat from D Price Butchers, whose acorn-fed pigs roam freely. In the heart of the New Forest, this comforting café is often a pit stop for cyclists, horse riders and tuk-tuk travellers (see ch. 95). These customers may not be able to buy any of the plants, bulbs or herbs for sale (unless they have great balance) but they could make use of the seed library if their green fingers start tingling.

Or they may choose to sit with Mother Nature on the patio while drinking in the vibrant blooms, herbaceous borders and thriving potager. They could even order a 'caffe mocha vodka valium latte', as is suggested on a sign hanging inside.

Opened in September 2019, it's not just the daytime fare that keeps diners satisfied. Evening events are also hosted, such as Fish on Fridays, Pie 'n' Pud Night, Tapas on the Terrace and a monthly supper club often serving international food – Italian, Mexican, Indian – using local produce.

Live music by local musicians is always a hit, too. This charming café offers good food and good times by the shedload.

Address Gorley Lynch, Fordingbridge SP6 2QB, +44 (0)1425 655392, www.pottingshedhyde.co.uk | **Getting there** By car, take Wessex Way, A338, A31, Salisbury Road, Ringwood Road, Lawrence Lane, Ringwood Road and Buddle Hill to Gorley Lynch | **Hours** Tue–Sun 10am–4pm (food served 10am–2.45pm) | **Tip** Prior to opening The Potting Shed, Lee owned The Compasses Inn in Damerham, about six miles away (www.compassesinndamerham.co.uk). A friendly pub with local, homemade food also at its core.

78 Priory Bell Tower
Ring the changes

Ding-dong, ding-dong… BONG! You may want to take your ear-plugs for the 90-minute Bell Tower Tour of Christchurch Priory. If you're in the belfry – where the huge copper and tin bells are housed – on the hour, half hour or quarter hour, you'll be blasted with the sound of the 1.5-ton tenor bell, plus four others, which are connected to the Priory's tower clock. For the full '12-bong' experience, time it for midday – then brace yourself!

Hung on a frame of New Forest oak, the 13 bells range in date from 1370 to 1976. Bells 9 and 10 were presented to the Priory by King Edward III and are among the oldest in the country still being rung regularly. Known as 'King's Head Bells', look closely and you'll see the king's head cast into the inscription.

Three other areas in the tower are visited during the tour, each accessed via the 176-step spiral stone staircase. Your first stop will be the north porch room, which accommodated the original seven bells, then became a hiding place for smuggled booze in the 18th and 19th centuries (see ch. 93). It's believed it was also used as a courtroom. Today it is Christchurch History Society's HQ, with a photo of the queen visiting the Priory in 1966 on display. The next stop is the ringing room, where you'll learn how the bells are rung (it's more complicated than you'd think) and see a plethora of peal boards, which record various peals (at least 5,040 'changes' in about three hours) rung at the Priory to mark significant events, such as the relief of Mafeking during the Boer War in 1900.

The finale of the tour is a visit to the 120-foot-high roof. The view is stunning, and on a clear day you may even see Salisbury Cathedral, some 25 miles away. You will also see the pinnacle that was replaced on the wonk after it fell down during a storm in 1990 (see ch. 63 Tip). This tour is fascinating, and well worth turning up for – with bells on.

Address Christchurch Priory, Quay Road, Christchurch BH23 1BU, +44 (0)1202 485804, www.christchurchpriory.org/visiting/priory-tours | **Getting there** Bus 1 or 1a to Priory Corner, then a 5-minute walk | **Hours** The belfry is only accessible on guided tours, which run Mar–Oct. Visit the website for details of how to book. | **Tip** Want to learn more about the Priory? The Cream Tea Tour will take you on a guided walk of the ground floor and crypt (including areas not open to the public), then into Cloisters Tea Rooms for scones and tea.

79 Pug's Hole
The smuggle is real

If you walk through this 10-acre wood during springtime, you may hear the *tap-tap-tap* of the great spotted woodpecker making its mark on one of the pine, hazel, rowan or sycamore trees. If, however, you'd have walked through this same wood in the 1700s, you may have heard the *thud-thud-thud* of dirt being shovelled on top of something in a ditch. Pug's Hole is said to be named after Captain Pug, a local smuggler who buried his loot here. Another local smuggler, Isaac Gulliver (see ch. 55), was also known to transport his illegal imports through Pug's Hole on his way to Kinson, a central area for smuggling activity.

Another theory of how the nature reserve got its name is that 'Pug' comes from 'Puck', the old term meaning 'mischievous spirit'. There's another small forest near Kinson called Puck's Dell. Well, those smugglers were nothing if not mischievous – when smuggling was at its most rife in Dorset, between 1714 and 1830, around 80,000 gallons of brandy would land on Bournemouth's shore each year, along with lashings of gin, rum and tobacco.

As well as seeing woodpeckers, you may also be fortunate enough to spot a goldcrest, the UK's smallest bird. At around only three and a half inches, you may want to bring your binoculars to take a closer look at the distinctive yellow stripe on its head.

Before 1816, the whole area, including the length of Glenferness Avenue, was mainly heathland. But this changed when Scots pine trees were planted in order to provide a cash crop, as the land was no good for farming. Apparently, the planters were so poorly paid that half the saplings were placed in the ground upside down. The large oak on the south side of the wooded valley predates this 19th-century pine plantation, but a large number of Scots pine trees remain in Pug's Hole today. The question is, though, is any of Captain Pug's treasure still here?

Address Glenferness Avenue, BH4 9ND | **Getting there** Bus m1, m2, 1 or 3 to Grosvenor Road, then a 15-minute walk. The main entrance is next to 7a Glenferness Avenue (Pine Lodge flats); the other entrance is at the back of Talbot Heath School on Rothesay Road | **Tip** Another local smuggler with his own 'Hole' is Samuel Hookey. The story goes that he fell into the River Stour trying to escape the revenue men and, weighed down by the gold he was carrying, sank into one of the holes in the riverbed. The gold is said to still be there, inside 'Hookey's Hole'.

80 'Red Joan's' Birthplace
Playing I spy

If you had to conjure an image of a female spy, what would you imagine? A *femme fatale* with killer wits and killer heels? Most likely, you wouldn't picture a great-grandmother with a vegetable allotment and a penchant for Co-op tea. But that's exactly what Melita Norwood was by the time her 40-plus years of espionage were discovered. The Soviet Union's longest-serving British spy, Melita began her life in Pokesdown, born in 1912 to a British mother and Latvian father. She had been part of the 'Tolstoy colony' living in Tuckton House, now the site of 9–17 Saxonbury Road (see ch. 43). Her bookbinder father helped to produce a radical newspaper that printed articles by Russian revolutionaries Trotsky and Lenin.

During World War II, Melita worked as secretary to a director at the British Non-Ferrous Metals Research Association, and was recruited by the KGB to pass secrets relating to the atomic bomb project – codenamed Tube Alloys – to them. In doing so, she shortened the Soviet Union's own atomic bomb project by up to five years. It wasn't until 1999, when Melita was 87, that her crime against her country was publicly revealed, by which time it was deemed 'inappropriate' to prosecute due to her age. The 2018 film *Red Joan*, starring Dame Judi Dench and Sophie Cookson, was based on Melita, the woman described as 'the most important British female agent in KGB history'.

Melita wasn't the only local spy though. Anthony Blunt from the Cambridge Five Spy Ring (who, incidentally, weren't nearly as valuable to the Soviet Union as Melita was) was born in Bournemouth, and Harry Houghton and Ethel Gee of Portland Spy Ring fame settled in Poole (living at 4 Brunstead Road) in the 1970s after their release from prison.

It seems the area has many past connections to espionage. Who knows, maybe it's still a hotbed for spooks. Do you *really* know what your neighbour does for a living?

Address Seabourne Road, Pokesdown BH7 6AX | **Getting there** Bus 1 or m2 to Pokesdown train station. The Pokesdown sign is opposite the station | **Tip** Take a 10-minute walk to The Crooked Book (725 Christchurch Road, BH7 6AQ) to see if they stock *The Spy Who Came in from the Co-op* by David Burke, a book about Melita. Or even *The Spy Who Came in from the Cold* by John Le Carré, who, incidentally, was born in Poole.

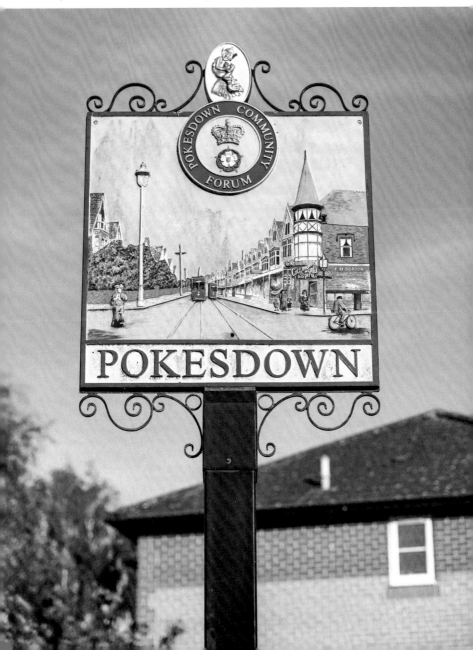

81 Regent Centre
Reeling the audiences in

'Saturday night at the movies, Who cares what picture you see, When you're huggin' with your baby, In the last row of the balcony?' When The Drifters sang this hit, they didn't warn young courters that right behind the last row of the balcony, there's a small window that someone working in the projector room can stick their head out of.

As part of the Regent Centre tour, you can stick your own head out of said window, in the now-defunct 'non-sync room'. In here sits a record player and collection of records, once played during films that needed music. You'll also watch trailers on the big screen, beamed out from an original 35-mm projector, which became obsolete in 2012, when the Regent went digital.

When the cinema opened on Boxing Day, 1931 (after being built in just five months for £25,000), it screened *The Taming of the Shrew* from such a projector – and recreated the experience on Boxing Day, 2021, to celebrate its 90-year anniversary.

While you're in the centre's museum – set up in 2017 – get lost in the silver screen's days of yore. You'll find velvet-covered seats with ashtrays attached to the back; a number of film reels stacked up, one labelled *Indiana Jones*; an Automaticket machine that will dispense a movie ticket for you; a strip of cinema screen with tiny holes in, which allow the sound to come through from the speakers behind (a typical screen has about 5,500 perforations per square foot); and vintage film posters, including one for the double bill of *The Thief Who Came to Dinner* and *The Train Robbers*, the last films to be shown here in 1973, when the cinema closed to become a bingo hall. It reopened as a cinema 10 years later.

You can also read about the history of several local cinemas: The Grand in Westbourne, The Ritz in Winton, The Regal in Parkstone, The Savoy in Boscombe… Sadly, these have all closed. But the Regent Centre lives on. What are you doing Saturday night?

Address 51 High Street, Christchurch BH23 1AS, +44 (0)1202 499199, www.regentcentre.co.uk | Getting there Bus 1, 1a or 1b to Christchurch town centre; half a mile from Christchurch train station | Hours Check the website for tour dates | Tip Another 1930s cinema to have withstood the test of time is the Tivoli Theatre in Wimborne (www.tivoliwimborne.co.uk).

82   Rolls Drive

Tragedy in the air

There is only one Rolls Drive in the UK – possibly the world. But then, there was only one Charles Rolls (co-founder of Rolls-Royce), whom this road is named after. The Hon. Charles Stewart Rolls was the first ever Briton to die in a powered-aircraft accident. On 12 July, 1910, while competing in Britain's first International Aviation Meeting at Southbourne Aerodrome, the tail of his Wright biplane failed to do its job properly, causing the machine to lose control and crash 80 feet to the ground, in front of a crowd of several thousands, killing the 32-year-old pioneer almost instantly.

A month before his sudden death, Rolls had become the first person ever to make a nonstop return crossing of the English Channel by plane, making him the best-known aviator in the country. He was also a racing driver, a balloonist, an adventurer, a businessman and a government advisor. The death of this national hero was so significant that parliamentary business at Westminster was interrupted to announce it.

Bournemouth is no stranger to disastrous aircraft displays. In 1919, the town hosted the ill-fated Schneider Trophy, which saw planes sink in the sea, get lost in the fog and flip over during take-off. Newspapers labelled the event 'a fiasco in the fog'. Information boards at Spyglass Point by Alum Chine tell the full sorry tale.

The site of Rolls' fatal crash is where the playing field of St Peter's School now is, and a memorial plaque for Rolls was placed here in 1978, then refurbished by Rolls-Royce in 2010, 100 years after he died. Every year, on the Saturday closest to 12 July – the anniversary of his death – a public commemorative service takes place here, organised by the Charles Rolls Heritage Trust.

The Trust is in the process of getting a heritage sculpture approved to sit in the more accessible vicinity of Hengistbury Head, possibly on Rolls Drive, so everyone can honour this high-flier.

Address Rolls Drive, Southbourne BH6 4NA | Getting there Bus 1 to Tuckton Bridge, then a 20-minute walk. Selfridge Avenue (see ch. 53) leads to Rolls Drive | Tip Not all airborne escapades went badly in Bournemouth. On 11 April, 1914, British aviator Gustav Hamel, who flew the world's first airmail flight, produced the world record of 21 loop the loops in his aircraft over Meyrick Park. And on 27 August, 1930, Amy Johnson, the first woman to fly solo from Britain to Australia, opened the Bournemouth Hospital Fête in Meyrick Park after landing her plane at Talbot Village.

83 Roma Italian Delicatessen
Mamma mia (*chef's kiss*)

Parmesan, roasted ham, marinated artichokes, a pasta dish, and soup or salad, depending on the time of year: pop into Roma Italian Delicatessen on a Tuesday and you might see local artist Bob Parks buying his weekly continental basics. Having lived in Sway in the New Forest for more than 35 years, the eccentric bohemian was a key part of the Los Angeles art scene in the early 1970s, and was often seen walking the streets in a string bikini. His equally wacky contemporaries included Chris Burden, who got someone to shoot him in the arm with a rifle, and Paul McCarthy, who smothered his naked body with ketchup in the name of art.

While Roma doesn't stock ketchup (thank goodness – who knows where it could end up!), you will find juicy San Marzano tomatoes and oil-drenched sun-dried tomatoes, as well as an abundance of other authentic Italian fare: olives, antipasto, porcini mushrooms, Sardinian bread, Calabrian hot chillies, dried pasta (including linguine with black squid ink and tagliolini with salmon), gelato, biscotti, cannoli, balsamic vinegar (including orange and lemon flavours), truffle cream, Aperol spritz in individual-serving bottles… and a selection of about 20 cold meats and 25 cheeses.

The homemade food on offer will also get your mouth watering. An ever-changing menu of dishes such as Angus beef lasagna (a bestseller); baked rigatoni with Tuscan sausages, pancetta and provolone cheese; and ravioli filled with asparagus and ricotta in a tomato and pesto sauce are prepared by owners Paolo – who is from Rome but has lived in Bournemouth since 1988 – and his wife Encarni, from Barcelona. They also whip up a creamy, dreamy tiramisu and three types of fresh pesto: mushroom, walnut and Genovese.

In 2016, *The R&B Feeling: The Bob Parks Story* aired on BBC Four. Why not stock up at Roma, then head home to find it on Vimeo, before indulging in an afternoon of art and artichokes?

Address 20 Church Street, Christchurch BH23 1BW, +44 (0)1202 488544 | Getting there Bus 1 or 1a to Priory Corner | Hours Mon–Sat 8.30am–4.30pm | Tip Treat yourself to one of the eight varieties of takeaway coffee to sip while strolling around the grounds of Christchurch Priory, a 30-second walk away.

84 Rustic Treats Bakery
Arrested development

Pop into this artisan bakery and while you're deciding between a sourdough loaf or a cinnamon bun, ponder what happened on these premises in August 1963, when the residents of the flat above were dealing with a quite different type of dough. Roger Cordrey and William Boal were staying in the three-bedroom flat above Mould's Florists – now Rustic Treats Bakery – laying low from the authorities who were searching for the culprits of the Great Train Robbery, a crime in which some £2.6 million (equivalent to about £55 million today) was stolen from a Royal Mail train heading from Glasgow to London.

The pair's game of hide-and-seek didn't last long; they were arrested on Tweedale Road six days after the robbery, following a tip-off from Ethel Clarke (a policeman's widow) who had been suspicious when they paid her three months' rent upfront, in used 10 shilling notes, to lease her garage. A total of about £141,000 was found in various locations around the area, with £56,000 in Ethel Clarke's garage, £79,000 in another garage on Ensbury Avenue, and £5,900 inside the flat – £5,060 in a briefcase and £840 under a pillow. A new car Cordrey and Boal had just bought, a Ford Anglia, was also found in the car park of the Horse and Jockey Hotel on Wimborne Road, with a copy of the *Bournemouth Echo* inside, featuring a front-page story about the robbery. Cordrey was jailed for 20 years, Boal for 24, but their sentences were reduced to 14 years each on appeal. Although Cordrey pleaded guilty, Boal maintained his innocence until he died in jail in 1970. Seeing as the mastermind of the crime, Bruce Reynolds, had never heard of Boal, it's probable he was telling the truth.

Rustic Treats Bakery opened in 2015 and serves delicious cakes, pastries and speciality breads and rolls, including sourdough, olive, spelt, rye and garlic. Forget the Great Train Robbery… how about some Great Grain Scoffery?

Address 935 Wimborne Road, Moordown BH9 2BN, +44 (0)7549 376013, www.facebook.com/rustictreatsbakery | Getting there Bus 5 or 5a to Ensbury Park Road, then a 7-minute walk | Hours Mon–Fri 8am–4.30pm, Sat 10am–1.30pm | Tip The most notorious criminal from the Great Train Robbery was Ronnie Biggs, who is said to have had connections in Bournemouth. He apparently knew the landlord of the Old Osprey pub on Poole Lane (now demolished and replaced with housing), and there was a card from him in a display case on the fireplace.

85 San Remo Towers
Up on the roof

Residents of this Grade II-listed complex will tell you that the roof is the best place to watch the annual Bournemouth Air Festival. During World War II, however, the aircraft overhead weren't so friendly, and the roof had a more ominous function. It housed anti-aircraft guns that brought down a German plane, plus Lewis machine guns. One of these weapons once fell from its stand, spraying bullets everywhere. The Luftwaffe (German Air Force) used San Remo Towers as a reference point.

In 1943, the government took over the building, allocating the top two floors to American or Canadian troops. The fifth-floor restaurant never opened to residents; instead, it became a canteen for the soldiers, with food sent up in a dumbwaiter that's now hidden behind the walls. In the 1950s, the restaurant was converted into a penthouse, number C53. The National Fire Service also occupied some flats and kept its fire engines in the garage.

Built between 1935–1938 and described as 'an exotic fantasy', the five blocks containing 183 flats are set in a U-shape around a courtyard. In 1939, rental prices ranged from £96 to £260 a year. Architect Hector Hamilton (who was a dollar millionaire at 26, before going bankrupt, then finding his feet again) used a Spanish mission style, with decorative features à gogo: colourful faience tiles (produced by Carter & Co., which Poole Pottery was originally part of), ornate pillars, barley-sugar columns, pantile roofing, terracotta motifs, detailed balustrades and bright door jambs. Inside, the corridors are now lined with monogrammed carpet, reminiscent of a cruise liner. The building's design is flamboyant and full of fun.

The social life of residents was also full of fun. Stories abound of the days when they'd don their diamonds and pearls to quaff champagne in the residents' lounge. This characterful building is steeped in history of the high life.

Address Sea Road, Boscombe BH5 1JT | Getting there Bus 1, 1a, 1b or m2 to Boscombe Crescent, then a 7-minute walk | Hours Viewable from the outside only | Tip Dotted along Sea Road, from Boscombe's shopping precinct to Boscombe Pier, there are seven sculptures as part of the Boscombe Arts Trail. The two closest to San Remo Towers are a huge marble trapped inside a bench and a giant metal feather commemorating Percy and Mary Shelley (see ch. 61).

86 Seagull & the Windbreak

Access all areas

Buckets and spades… Ice creams… Beach balls… Just a few things associated with the seaside. Seagulls and windbreaks also top the list, which are what inspired Peter Francis-Lewis and a:b:i:r architects when they entered the 2009 competition to design the UK's first beach huts built specifically for people with disabilities. Out of 173 entries from all over the world, their concept – including a 'line-drawn' seagull as the canopy roof and curved multicoloured stripes to represent a windbreak – won, and the four beach huts were opened on 24 August, 2011 by members of community-interest company DOTS Disability.

Built as part of the Boscombe Sea Change regeneration scheme, and costing £115,000, all of the beach huts can accommodate up to four wheelchair users. With a total floor area of 147-feet-squared, there are height-adjustable kitchen units, plus bright, high-contrast surfaces and floors to help those who are visually impaired. An electric charging point for mobility scooters is also available. Outside the huts, between May and September, mats are laid on the sand to allow wheelchair users to access the beach and sea more easily.

Various other local places have considered how to enhance the experience of people with special needs. Firefighters at Christchurch Fire Station have turned their allotment into a sensory garden for those with physical and learning disabilities; Monkey World has a 'sensory statue' of an orangutan's head to give visually impaired visitors an idea of the size and shape of the ape's face; Dorset Museum houses a hands-on fossil exhibition with descriptive audio guide for visually impaired people, as well as a Calm Space where those with autism (for example) can get away from crowds and noise; and Elwood Cottages in Blandford are fully set up for people in wheelchairs – not a step in sight.

Being 'accessible' doesn't just mean having a disabled toilet.

Address Boscombe Seafront, Undercliff Drive, Boscombe BH5 1BN, +44 (0)1202 123800, www.bournemouth.co.uk/things-to-do/accessible-beach-huts-p2234983 | Getting there Bus 1a to Boscombe Gardens. From Boscombe Pier, if you're looking at the beach, turn right and it's less than a minute away. | Hours The beach huts are available for hire all year round. | Tip For a fun, easy way to reach the beach from the clifftop – and back again – use one of the funicular railway cliff lifts (West Cliff Lift or Fisherman's Walk Cliff Lift). They're wheelchair-accessible, as are the Land Trains that run along the prom.

87 Setley Ridge Vineyard

The grape outdoors

Have you noticed that most bottles of wine don't list the ingredients on the label? If they did, wine lovers might put down their glass in disgust and reach for some water instead. It's not uncommon for wine to contain fish bladders, animal blood, bone marrow and arsenic (yes, really!). But, fear not, when you drink one of the four wines produced at Setley Ridge Vineyard (dry white, dry rosé, oaked red and the occasional sparkling), rest assured they are vegan and won't poison you.

While no nasties are added here, certain solutions are needed to balance the flavour and acidity of the wine. Sugar is also added, which boosts the alcohol content – a process called chaptalisation. Paul Girling – who opened Setley Ridge with his wife Hayley in 2001 (they tied the knot amongst the vines in 2006) – buys about half a tonne of sugar every year for this purpose. He raised eyebrows in 2020 when fellow shoppers thought he was jumping on the pandemic panic-buying bandwagon.

On the 60-to-90-minute tour, Paul walks visitors around part of the six-acre property, encouraging them to eat a juicy grape or two from one of the 7,000 vines as they go. He talks through the process of growing, pruning and hand-harvesting the fruit, explaining that they don't use pesticides, opting instead for predatory insects to keep pests at bay. As such, there's a thriving array of wildlife here, including deer, badgers, foxes, toads, snakes and birds (the vines are netted so the birds don't completely ransack them). A veritable Farthing Wood! In autumn, after the grapes have been harvested, Paul brings in around 50 sheep to offer some 'natural fertilisation' to the land. Three woolly workmates – Marge, Gloria and Penelope – act as lawn mowers throughout the year.

After the tour has finished, head to the farm shop, where you can buy one (or several) of the 6,000 to 8,000 bottles of wine the vineyard produces each year. Cheers!

Address Lymington Road, Brockenhurst SO42 7UF, +44 (0)1590 622246, www.setleyridge.co.uk | Getting there Just over a mile from Brockenhurst train station | Hours Tours run from spring to autumn. Farm shop opening hours: Mon–Sat 9am–5pm, Sun 10am–4pm | Tip More of a beer person? Head next door to microbrewery Pig Beer (www.pigbeer.com).

88 Shell Christchurch Priory
All washed up

She sells seashells by the seashore… then they get cleaned, sorted and made into a miniature replica of Christchurch Priory. Created around 1960 by German woodcarver Werner Rolls, this model was originally on display in Mulley's China Shop (now Spirit Hair Design) on Bridge Street, before it found its home in the Red House Museum.

Rolls had been a soldier during World War II, based in Jersey, but was taken prisoner during a commando raid and brought to England. After the war, he remained here and worked in the Purewell Building Works in Christchurch. He found time to craft this 9-inch (height) by 16-inch (length) by 7-inch (depth) micro model of Christchurch Priory, which, at 311 feet itself, is the longest parish church in England. Rolls used about 4,000 shells and carved wooden furniture to go inside, which was later lost.

Something else that has been lost – from which Rolls perhaps took some inspiration – is the Shell House in Southbourne. With two grottos, a church, several shrines, a wishing well and a statue of Saint George and the Dragon, it consisted of more than a million shells from all over the world, plus the largest shell in Britain. Locals and tourists alike remember this quirky attraction fondly, which existed from 1948 to 2001, when it was demolished (a block of flats now stands in its place).

Prior to this, the house had been called Heathercliff and was owned by Major-General Sir Owen Tudor Burne, who was abundantly decorated for his service in India during the Indian Mutiny. A double tragedy occurred at the house in April 1878 when his mother and wife both died there. Burne is buried at Christchurch Priory.

We've come full circle. As you look at this pint-sized Priory, take a moment to ponder what the owner of The Shell House, George Howard, once said: 'Shells are the only things in this world that grow more beautiful after death'.

Address Red House Museum and Gardens, Quay Road, Christchurch BH23 1BU, +44 (0)1202 482860, www.hampshireculture.org.uk/red-house-museum-and-gardens | **Getting there** Bus 1 or 1a to Priory Corner. The model is in the garden, past the café's seating. | **Hours** Wed – Sun 10am – 4pm | **Tip** Next to the Shell Christchurch Priory you'll see *The Nimbus*, the oldest salmon punt in the country, built specifically with a flat bottom to navigate Christchurch Harbour's shallow water. The Shell Priory is missing the salmon weather vane that sits atop the real Christchurch Priory, commemorating the fact that the first salmon caught every year was always given to the Prior.

89 Silent Yoga UK
The pursuit of peacefulness

Forget about the dishes in the sink, your never-ending to-do list and that meeting with your boss; Silent Yoga is all about drowning out the world. Chilled-out tunes and the soothing voice of an instructor are transmitted through wireless headphones; think 'silent disco' but replace embarrassing shape throwing on the dance floor with flowing yoga poses on the beach.

Having grown in popularity in the US and Australia, Silent Yoga UK was set up in Bournemouth in 2017. As well as sessions all over town – Boscombe Beach, Ashley Cross Green, Alum Chine Beach, Picnic Park Deli (see ch. 74) – the headphoned yogis hit up events up and down the country, including Camp Bestival, Camp Wildfire, Flo Vibe and Neverworld. They also host Silent Yoga parties and private events, like birthday celebrations and 'zen hen dos'.

It seems no two sessions are the same. The instructors, Anna and Sabrina, bring their own unique twist to each class, with varying yoga styles and poses for all abilities. Many of the classes are themed and it's as much about the 'experience' as the yoga itself – as those who attended the Fireworks Silent Yoga Disco will attest. Ever watched the sky light up through your legs of a downward dog? Add it to your bucket list! Or you may want to try Yoga in the Dark, where zen-seekers are blindfolded.

The Nidra Under the Stars session is also quite an experience. Held in winter, those wanting relaxation, enlightenment and a kip on the beach snuggle into their sleeping bag with hot-water bottle inside, while incense wafts and candles flicker, and allow their minds to be taken on a journey (by the instructor's voice through their headphones) to a magical, tranquil place – think snow-capped mountains and crystal-clear lakes. This guided meditation inspires yogic sleep, the state of consciousness between waking and sleeping. It's seriously calming and sure beats counting sheep.

Address Yoga sessions are held at various locations, +44 (0)7714 761379 or +44 (0)7716 689582, www.facebook.com/silentyogauk | Tip Want more yoga? Check out Park Yoga, held in Bournemouth Central Gardens (www.parkyoga.co/bournemouth).

90 Sir Arthur Conan Doyle's Grave

Put that in your pipe

Sherlock Holmes: synonymous with a deerstalker hat, the catch-phrase 'Elementary, my dear Watson' (despite the fact that the private detective never actually uttered this phrase in the four novels and 56 short stories in which he appeared), a magnifying glass and a pipe. The latter two can be found on the grave of the sleuth's creator, author Sir Arthur Conan Doyle, in All Saints Churchyard in Minstead. Occasionally, the props go missing so are replaced by a kind parishioner on regular 'pipe watch'.

Doyle is described on his gravestone as a 'Patriot, Physician & Man of Letters'. An agnostic, he was also a spiritualist, which didn't sit too well with the Church of England but, ever willing to compromise, they agreed he could be buried in this graveyard, albeit by the far boundary under an oak tree. Shortly after he was buried in 1955 (having been reinterred here from his estate in Crowborough), this tree was struck by lightning, then again in 1969. Could it be that God was trying to make a point?

Although Doyle lived in East Sussex, he bought a rural retreat called Bignell Wood near Minstead in which he would relax, unwind and… hold séances. Apparently, Charles Dickens once 'came through' and asked the writer to complete his unfinished works! The New Forest, and Minstead in particular, feature strongly in Doyle's novel *The White Company*. As does Christchurch Castle, originally Twynham Castle. The castle ruins can be seen from Church Hatch in Christchurch, a Georgian property that Doyle stayed at around 1891. Inspiration for *The Adventure of the Speckled Band* (Doyle's favourite Sherlock Holmes short story) was also sparked at this residence. Now a Grade II-listed townhouse, in 2016 it was put on the market for £1.5 million. Expensive, my dear readers.

Address All Saints Church, Church Close, Minstead, Lyndhurst SO43 7EX | Getting there By car, take Wessex Way then A31 to Minstead; about 6 miles from Ashurst New Forest train station | Tip Doyle also dabbled in architecture and sketched the designs for a third-storey extension and an alteration of the front façade of the Lyndhurst Grand Hotel (later Lyndhurst Park Hotel). Located at 78 High Street in Lyndhurst, plans to demolish the building were set in motion in 2014, but when these original sketches from 1912 were discovered, the building was saved.

91 The Smugglers Wain
On the wagon

Wondering why *The Smugglers Wain* looks familiar? If you've been to The National Gallery, you may have seen the painting that inspired it, John Constable's 1821 *The Hay Wain*. One of the most iconic paintings in the history of British art, it's also possible you've seen it on a placemat or biscuit tin.

Created in 2010 by David Harbott, and measuring 36 feet by 23 feet, *The Smugglers Wain* depicts elements of Kinson's history, with the smuggling industry of the 1700s a focal point. The artwork is composed of a compilation of images, old and new, with some 3,000 photos having been sifted through to select the ones you see. The central wain – or cart – is surrounded by people and buildings significant to the area. To its left is St Andrew's Church (see ch. 93), where smugglers stashed their contraband; and on the far left are two of the 108 Lady Wimborne Cottages built between 1867 and 1904 for the local farm labourers. Towering over these is the 'Kinson Oak', the tree at the junction of East Howe Lane and Wimborne Road, marking the boundary between Kinson and Ensbury. Speaking of boundaries, Kinson almost became part of Poole in 1931, but a campaign by residents saw the area added to Bournemouth, with the boundaries extended to also include Holdenhurst and Wallisdown.

To the right of the wain are gypsy wagons. These travellers would set up camp in the parish in quirky-sounding areas such as Cuckoo Bottom, Monkeys Hump, Sugar Knob Mountain, Frying Pan, Bribery Island and Wallywack. The white building on the far right is the 1788 Pelhams House, which was extended in 2004 to include Kinson Community Centre. Community has always been central to the area; whether it was pre-Domesday Book dwellers, farmers, smugglers, gypsies, traders, the two men about to cut the grass or the children dangling their legs from the bridge in this mural, Kinson's 'togetherness' is what sets it apart.

Address The Kinson Hub, Wimborne Road, Kinson BH11 9AW | Getting there Bus 5a to The Kinson Hub. The mural is on the back wall of the building. | Tip Walk around the building and you'll see an information board titled 'The Changing Names of Kinson'. In 1086 the area was called Chinestanestone, in 1326 it became Kenstaneton, then in 1662 it was Kynston, before becoming Kingston How in 1771, until it landed on Kinson in 1800. Then go inside the building to see the annotated display of *The Smugglers Wain*.

92 SRDE Platform
Giving off the right signals

Did the night-vision scene in *Silence of the Lambs* give you night-mares? You've got the work carried out here in the late 1950s to thank for that. As well as researching and developing optical fibres, mine detectors, and satellite and battlefield communications using radar, the Ministry of Defence's Signals Research and Development Establishment (SRDE) – based at Friars Cliff from the early days of World War II to 1980 – also conducted much of the initial research on night-vision equipment. To assist the programme, a 330-foot tunnel was constructed at Steamer Point, in which the lighting would be controlled to simulate varying levels of darkness. Of course, the technology was developed for military purposes rather than freaking out moviegoers.

This concrete platform, although now used for ball games and skateboarding, once had a more important role. It was the site of the first British military communications satellite station, and received and transmitted signals from the first British-launched military satellite – as well as foreign satellites. An aerial dish 40 feet in diameter sat on top of the platform and other dishes sat on the smaller concrete plinths nearby. To protect the dishes from the elements, radomes (resembling mini Epcot Centers) covered them.

Two similar structures were built in Singapore and Cyprus and formed the beginning of the worldwide military-communication satellite system Skynet (no, not the artificial-intelligence system of the same name that sent killing machines back in time to wreak havoc, as in the *Terminator* films). Skynet helps British troops – and our allies – around the globe.

The research carried out at this site was groundbreaking, and extended beyond military advancements. You've likely encountered it many times – like if you've watched cable TV, had an MRI scan… or seen Jodie Foster being stalked by a psycho in the dark.

Address Penny Way, Friars Cliff, Christchurch BH23 4TA | Getting there Bus 1a to Hoburne Park, then a 10-minute walk; if driving, park in Steamer Point Car Park and the platform is on the green across the road | Tip Walk to Steamer Point Nature Reserve and you'll find the spot (marked by a sign titled *The Steamer*) where, in 1829, a paddle steamer was wedged into a cliff opening so it could be used as a site office for those building nearby Highcliffe Castle (see ch. 53). This is how the area got its name.

93 St Andrew's Church Tower

At the end of their rope

If you want to hide something, where do you stash it? Under your bed? In the shed? In the biscuit tin? If you were a smuggler in the 1700s, you may have opted for this ironstone rubble tower, which dates back to around 1100. Notorious smuggler Isaac Gulliver (see ch. 55) and his cronies would heave-ho kegs of liquor onto the top of this tower, and the grooves on the parapets made by the ropes can still be seen. They would store silk, lace and tea contraband in the tower too, as well as in fake tombs in the churchyard. The Oakely tomb can be seen in front of the church, although it was positioned elsewhere in the smuggling days. A tunnel is also said to run underground, which smugglers would use as an escape route when needs be.

In 1904, the clock on the tower was added in memory of Queen Victoria. Having been partial to a whisky or two, perhaps she would have been thrilled to be associated with this once liquor-laden tower.

Another local hidey-hole was Christchurch Priory, where smugglers would haul barrels of booze up, up, and tuck them away (see ch. 78). Rope marks can also be seen here, near the north porch room. The locals who were 'in on' this activity would wave a lantern to warn the smugglers of any problems, and this lantern is now in the Priory's museum.

The churchyard at St Andrew's is the resting place for many smugglers and their relatives. Isaac Gulliver's daughter, Elizabeth, is buried in the Fryer family tomb, having married William Fryer. Robert Trotman's grave reads: *To the memory of Robert Trotman… Who was barbarously murder'd on the shore near Poole the 24th March 1765. A little tea one leaf I did not steal, For guiltless blood shed I to God appeal, Put tea in one scale human blood in t'other, And think what tis to slay thy harmless brother.* Was he, as his headstone suggests, innocent of smuggling tea, or did the excise men get their guy?

Address Millhams Road, Kinson BH10 7LN, +44 (0)1202 570010, www.standrewskinson.org | Getting there Bus 5 or 5a to The Kinson Hub | Tip Two of Isaac Gulliver's great-grandchildren, Sir John Fryer and Ada Augusta Russell, were prominent benefactors of St Andrew's Church. The nearby roads Fryer Close and Russell Road are named after them.

94 St Catherine's Hill

The grass is greener

St Catherine's Hill has points of interest aplenty. The stunning views across the Avon Valley… The nuclear bunker built during the Cold War, designed so three men could survive inside for up to three weeks… The discoveries made, including animal remains from the Ice Age, implements dating back to before 6,800 B.C. and an Iron Age animal pound… The two reservoirs that provide Christchurch and West Hampshire with water, each holding two million gallons… The training ground for troops during the Crimean and both world wars… The Bronze Age burial grounds… And, er, this patch of grass.

Previously the site of a chapel from where the hill gets its name, the building was dedicated to the 4th-century martyr St Catherine. Built prior to 1302 – perhaps to displace the pagan worship on the hill – the chapel was likely demolished during the dissolution of the monasteries in 1539. The rest of the 86 acres of St Catherine's Hill consist of heathland, woodland and shrubland, supported by the acidic sandy soils. This patch, however, remains affected by the limestone foundations of the chapel, which alter the pH of the soil, meaning that grass can thrive here.

On this same site, before the chapel was built, was a Roman fort serving as a military two-way signal station, both a lookout and a beacon. The outline of the station can still be seen. A dig in 1967 found medieval stained glass, marble flooring, seven types of building stone and eight different roof tiles. This mishmash of materials suggests the chapel needed many alterations and repairs over the years, plus it may have been constructed from 'leftovers' – perhaps from Christchurch Priory.

The Priory was going to be built on St Catherine's Hill but legend has it that all the materials kept being mysteriously moved overnight to the site of the present Priory. Finally, the builders took this as a 'sign' and built it where it now stands.

Address Christchurch BH23 2NL (there are various entrances) | **Getting there** Around 1.5 miles from Christchurch train station. Use the entrance on Hillside Drive. Walk up the hill, turn right down the path before the five water valve marker posts, until you reach a bench dedicated to Tom Davies on your right and a concrete structure on your left. The grass patch is just past the structure. It's about a 10-minute walk. | **Tip** In the nearby Bunker Cafe & Bar (www.thebunkercafe.co.uk) learn more about St Catherine's Hill's varied history with the timeline on display, running from the Bronze Age to present day.

95 Take a Tuk Tuk
Living the Thai life

If you've been to Thailand, you'll know that tuk-tuks are a dime a dozen there. In the New Forest, however, not so much. Here, if you go for a spin in one of these quirky three-wheeled vehicles, you'll be greeted with surprised smiles, amused chuckles and envious waves. You'll also be met with horses, cows, donkeys, pheasants… and a stunning view from Castle Hill (pictured), which showcases the River Avon, lush pastures and the grand Breamore House in the distance.

Having never before seen a tuk-tuk, when owner Shaun Manston saw two in the space of a week in 2017 (one a disused mobile coffee shop and one on a surfing trip in Cornwall), he felt that the tuk-tuk gods – or fate – were telling him he needed these motorised rickshaws in his life. He bought the Take a Tuk Tuk business from the owner in Cornwall and relocated it to the New Forest. Despite pouring rain and his tuk-tuk breaking down during his first job at a fundraising event, Shaun recovered from his 'What am I doing?!' doubts and things have run far more smoothly since. His three tuk-tuks (each holding six passengers and able to get up to a speed of 45 miles per hour) are available to hire for weddings, proms, parties, pub crawls and guided tours.

Many a hill is visited on these tours, including the aforementioned Castle Hill; Blissford Hill, Hampshire's steepest slope (hold onto your hat!); and Deadman Hill, so-called as this was where wrongdoers were hanged and left as a warning to others. You'll also be taken to Stoney Cross, a dead-straight road formerly used as a World War II airfield (see ch. 4), and past Breamore Railway Station, which closed in 1964 – navigating over cattle grids, around windy back roads and through quaint villages.

Shaun will tailor your tour to suit you, offering local knowledge and making stop offs (pint at The Fighting Cocks?) as you go. A fun jaunt with a touch of Asian adventure.

Address Pick-up is usually outside The Gourmet Grocer, 71a High Street, Fordingbridge SP6 1AS, +44 (0)7534 259006, www.takeatuktuk.co.uk | Getting there Bus X3 to Fordingbridge Post Office | Hours Easter to end of Sept (weather dependent) | Tip Embrace Thai culture even more with Bournemouth's Thai Summer Fair held every August at King's Park, and Poole's Magic of Thailand Festival at Harbourside Park.

96__ Talbot Heath Bunker
Taking cover

Fire drills… Errands for the teacher… Dentist appointments… Children often love an excuse to get out of lessons. But, between 1939 and 1945, when pupils at Talbot Heath School were asked to leave their desks and head towards one of the four underground bunkers on the 22-acre school grounds, it was less 'exciting', more 'terrifying'.

Each 66-foot-long by 6-foot-wide air-raid shelter held up to 125 pupils and staff members during Luftwaffe bombing raids in World War II. They were used extensively, day and night – with pupils sleeping on the cold, comfortless wooden benches.

During the war, there were 51 air raids and around 960 air-raid warnings in Bournemouth, with more than 2,200 bombs falling on the town, killing around 350 people and damaging or destroying about 14,000 buildings.

Nearly seven decades later, one of these bunkers was restored. In 2011, in time for the school's 125th anniversary, it was emptied of the wooden chairs and desks that were being stored inside, and revamped to become a 'living classroom', where students now learn all about life during the war. The dugout has also been used in artistic photo shoots and videos.

The entrance to the bunker displays names of those who donated towards the refurbishment, many of whom are past students. Well, 'once a TH girl, always a TH girl', so says the all-girl school's website. Founded in 1886, a sense of pride still runs through Talbot Heath's corridors, first established by its original headmistress Mary Broad. Leading the school for 39 years, she was a high-spirited educationalist, shocking Victorian Bournemouth by taking her girls on nature rambles, where they'd 'behave with the abandon of boys'. This girl-power pluck remains; in 2018, Talbot Heath launched a branch of the United Nations Girl Up Foundation, which campaigns for the rights of girls around the world.

Address Talbot Heath School, Rothesay Road, Talbot Woods, BH4 9NJ, +44 (0)1202 761881, www.talbotheath.org | Getting there Bus m1 or m2 to Grosvenor Road, then a 20-minute walk | Hours Viewing strictly by arrangement, contact office@talbotheath.org. Open during Dorset Architectural Heritage Week, contact dahw@edht.org.uk | Tip Inside the bunker, information about Bournemouth in World War II is displayed, including the fact that Pilot Officer Cecil Henry Hight was killed in action on 15 August, 1940. Half a mile away, on the corner of Leven Avenue and Walsford Road, is a memorial stone at the site of his fatal crash.

97 — Talbot Village Almshouses
Sister act

Serena and Venus Williams… Pippa and Kate Middleton… The Brontës… There are many famous sisters in the world. While Georgina and Marianne Talbot may not be as well known as Serena et al., they certainly made their mark in Bournemouth. Horrified at the town's poverty, they used the inheritance from their father's death to help. Between 1850 and 1870, the philanthropic siblings funded the creation of 19 cottages (spaced along what is now Wallisdown Road, of which 16 remain), a school, a church, six farms, areas of woodland and these almshouses – collectively Talbot Village.

This row of seven Romanesque almshouses – once housing the elderly or widowed, now private residences – had a privy and a pigsty each, plus a communal well, which still stands on the driveway. On the building's front, note the Latin phrase *Laus Deo* – 'praise be to God' – above the 1862 date and shout-out to Georgina Charlotte Talbot. St Mark's Primary School, built in the same year, sits next door and has grown from its original capacity of 63 students to today's 420. Both buildings were designed by Christopher Crabb Creeke (see ch. 103), who was largely responsible for the early development of Bournemouth.

Of the six farms set up to offer employment and trade for the village, only one remains operational – Highmoor Farm, home to Zeus the bull and his harem of Highland cattle. This, however, is under threat from development, just as the others were (Talbot Village Farm became Bournemouth's first airfield in 1915, then later Bournemouth University).

The Talbot sisters set up the Talbot Village Trust, which continues the charitable work they began. One of the area's leading benefactors, it donates up to £1 million a year to local causes. For Georgina and Marianne, it was never a case of 'sisters are doin' it for themselves'; it was, and continues to be, that sisters are doin' it for others.

Address 1–7 Almshouses, Slades Lane, Talbot Village, BH10 4JA | **Getting there** Bus 6 or 17 to St Mark's and St Saviour's Church, then a 5-minute walk | **Tip** Visit St Mark's and St Saviour's Church (Wallisdown Road, BH10 4HY) to see the two memorial crosses for the Talbot sisters. Georgina died in 1870, around the time the church was completed, and its dedication was brought forward so she could be buried here.

98 Tank Track Marks
Hitting a brick wall

'When you see a tank, get into someone's garden, out of the way, as they don't steer very well.' This was the advice given to children by concerned parents during World War II, as training for D-Day occurred all over town. Tanks trundling along roads was a common sight and, looking at this scuffed wall on the road leading to Avon Beach – previously known as The Peep – it's clear that the parents' concern wasn't unwarranted. Made by a Sherman tank, the veering driver left his permanent mark here in the form of a damaged pier of bricks and track marks along the wall.

Other troops to have left their permanent mark in town while waiting for D-Day were Canadian soldiers Fortin, Boivin and A. Robinson, who etched their names, ranks and the date into some bricks inside Lansdowne House when they were staying there in April 1944. None of these names appear on the Commonwealth War Graves Commission's Debt of Honour Register, meaning they made it out of the war alive.

Thousands of other Allied troops – including at least 10,000 Canadians – were billeted to Bournemouth, put up in 70 different requisitioned hotels and buildings, including Bath Hill Court, Burlington Hotel, East Cliff Court Hotel and San Remo Towers (see ch. 85). An autograph book was found at the Madacas Hotel and includes a poem written by the 'men of the seventy third'. In part, it reads, 'We knew we had a job, A job that was tough and grim, Did we moan or shirk or quit? No – we bore it all with a grin'.

The troops' bravery before D-Day was commended in an official letter written by General Dwight D. Eisenhower, dropped on local beaches, stating, 'The eyes of the world are upon you… I have full confidence in your courage, devotion to duty and skill in battle. We will accept nothing less than full Victory! Good luck!'. In light of all the soldiers did for us, there's no hard feelings about the wall.

Address Mudeford, Christchurch BH23 4AN | **Getting there** By car, follow signs for Avon Beach; bus X1 to Bure Lane, then a 5-minute walk. The wall is on the right-hand side of the road leading to the beach. | **Tip** The construction of tank traps, gun emplacements and pillboxes around the area made Christchurch an 'anti-tank island', meaning the advancement of German forces would have been hindered due to these measures. A pillbox is still standing in Mudeford Wood, about a 5-minute drive from these tank track marks.

99 Thomas Johnson's Grave
His life mattered

'Shake hands – the black won't come off!' said minister Thomas Lewis Johnson to Bournemouth locals who may never have seen a black person up close. He moved to the town around 1894, after spending 28 years as a slave in Virginia in the US (he was freed in 1865, at the end of the Civil War) and time in Africa as a missionary. He lived at 66 Paisley Road, which he named 'Liberia' as a nod to his experiences in Africa, with his second wife Sarah, also a freed American slave. Preaching in churches and the YMCA, he'd show shackles and a whip, and a photo of him holding them was sold as a postcard to raise funds for missionary work.

Johnson died in 1921, at the age of 85, and was buried in the non-conformist section of East Cemetery. His grave was dug nine feet deep so Sarah could also be interred here after her death but, for reasons unknown, that never happened.

Dorset has a dark history with the slave trade, with black people arriving at a number of ports. The wealth from slave ownership – in this country or on plantations abroad – often funded a life of luxury, and when slavery was abolished in the UK in 1833, owners received compensation. John Erle-Drax, an ancestor of South Dorset MP Richard Drax, was paid £4,293 12s 6d – worth £3 million today – for the release of 189 slaves. The White-White family of Mudeford House owned slaves, and a whip is said to have hung on one of the walls as a memento. The fusee chain industry (see ch. 48) may also have had its roots in slavery.

Johnson's autobiography *Twenty-Eight Years a Slave* – also published as *The Story of My Life in Three Continents* – was first printed in 1882, then again in 1908, by then on its eighth edition. It's still in print. This incredible man, who endured decades of mistreatment, then travelled the world to spread the word of God and campaign against slavery, deserved to be shaken warmly by the hand.

Address East Cemetery, Plot Q2/95, Gloucester Road, Boscombe BH7 6LD, +44 (0)1202 526238, www.bournemouth.gov.uk/bereavement | Getting there Bus 1 or m2 to Parkwood Road. About half a mile from Pokesdown train station. From the main entrance, walk (or drive) down the path to the chapel. From the bench outside the front of it, the grave is 16 rows back, the third one in. | Hours The cemetery opens at 9am and closes at different times depending on the month; see the website for details | Tip Also in East Cemetery are the graves of 120 soldiers who died in World War I and 68 who died in World War II. Some are scattered throughout the burial ground but many are on a special plot just off the main path. A memorial for two soldiers who drowned off the coast of Bournemouth in January 1915, whose bodies were never recovered, is also there.

100 Throop Mill

Flour power

Previously a coeliac's worst nightmare, the once thriving Throop Mill is now an abandoned building used as a focal point for dog walkers, ramblers, anglers and cyclists navigating their way along part of the 64-mile Stour Valley Way. Thanks to the six sluice gates, which regulated the flow of water to the mill (and can be seen from the nearby bridge – look for the rusty cogs), the building was granted Grade II-listed status in 1975. This might be one of the reasons why all ideas to convert it into a residence, heritage centre, tea room, museum or craft centre have hit a brick wall.

Although the four-storey mill's red-brick walls may look a little crumbly in places, the building is solid and has been standing strong since around 1850. The foundations of an earlier building were discovered inside, which could be the base of the mill that was recorded here in William the Conqueror's 1086 Domesday Book. At that time, it was valued at 76 pence.

The mill has produced flour for many products over the years, including hardtack, or ships' biscuits, which were a staple for Tudor sailors on long voyages. At one time, the machinery allowed the production of 26 different grades of flour, including wholemeal, semolina and white. During World War II, production at Throop Mill was stepped up and flour was sent to field bakeries, which provided bread for the troops, in Portsmouth, Bovington and Tidworth.

Although Parsons & Sons sold the mill to Heygates in 1957, its name remains on the front of the building. The last miller to have worked here was Cecil Biles, who died on the top floor at the age of 82, while painting a window. He had worked here for more than 50 years and was faithful to the end.

No one knows the fate of this derelict pile but, despite still containing much of its milling equipment, it seems its flour-production days are over. This mill has had its run.

Address Throop Road, BH8 0DW | **Getting there** Bus 4 to John Pound House, then a 10-minute walk. To reach the River Stour and walk round the back of the mill, from Throop Mill Car Park, walk past the mill and turn left when you see a sign for Stour Valley Way Merritown Loop. | **Tip** Another local watermill is Place Mill on Christchurch Quay, BH23 1BY, which takes its water supply from the River Avon and, after powering the waterwheel, flows into the River Stour. It stopped grinding corn in 1908 and now serves as an art gallery.

101 Tibetan Buddhist Centre

Keep karma and carry on

Are you ready to be enlightened? Then head to the Sakya Thubten Ling Tibetan Buddhist Centre, where you can clear your mind with meditation, learn about Buddhist teachings and engage in the spiritual practice of sadhana. The centre, which welcomes Buddhists and non-Buddhists alike, was opened on 6 May, 2004 by Tibetan monk Venerable Lama Jamyang Lekshey, who visits every year to run Buddhist higher-teaching sessions, imparting his wisdom through guidance that is thousands of years old.

Other lamas (Tibetan Buddhist monks who have achieved the highest level of spiritual development) associated with this centre include His Holiness Sakya Trizin, who is second in seniority only to the Dalai Lama himself, the spiritual head of Tibetan Buddhism. In 2000, Sakya Trizin visited from India and addressed an audience of around 1,000 at the Bournemouth International Centre (BIC) and, in 2007, during his month-long stay, he packed out Bourne-mouth University's theatre with people from all over the world.

A gold Gautama Buddha is the focal point inside this oasis of calm, surrounded by all manner of meaningful, symbolic and fasci-nating items, like the Manjushri statue wielding a sword, which is said to cut through ignorance; an array of Buddhist texts rolled in yellow silk (yellow symbolises humility and separation from a mate-rialistic society); and a collection of blue candles, representing the Medicine Buddha. Visitors are encouraged to light one for anyone they know who is ill or suffering.

If you want to discover the True Meaning of Life, pop to the loo, where a wall hanging will tell you: 'If you contribute to other people's happiness, you will find the true goal'. Buddhism promotes respect, love, compassion, mindfulness, awareness and tranquillity, while uplifting the mind, body and spirit. If this sounds enticing, perhaps it's time you joined the Buddhahood.

Address Sakya Thubten Ling Tibetan Buddhist Centre, 167 Shelbourne Road, Charminster BH8 8RD, +44 (0)1202 538108, www.stl.org.uk | Getting there Bus m1 or 5a to The Richmond Arms, then a 6-minute walk | Hours Check the website as session times vary | Tip From good, honest people to good, honest food. Head to the nearby Etna Italian Restaurant for lip-smacking pizza and pasta (www.etnaitalianrestaurant.co.uk).

102 Town Hall

A spirited place

This building holds records of all births, deaths and marriages to have occurred in the borough since 1837. Converted into the town hall in 1921, it particularly focuses on the deaths, apparently being one of the area's most haunted buildings. Many paranormal beings have been seen, including a World War I soldier, thought to be Gerald Hoare, nephew of Bournemouth MP Brigadier General Henry Page Croft; a World War I nurse roaming the corridors, said to have jumped from the building after the death of one of her patients; and a headless maharaja sitting on a chair made from Indian teak, repurposed from a coffin, on the fourth floor.

They hail from the time when the building was used as a military hospital between 1914 and 1919. It was initially used for wounded Indian soldiers, then – after the withdrawal of the Indian Army Corps from France – became a British military hospital, also admitting Australian and New Zealand troops. Originally opened as the high-class Hotel Mont Dore in 1885, the Turkish baths were used as a mortuary as they were the ideal shape for bodies.

Needle, plunge, pine, medicated and seawater baths also formed part of the spa facilities, as well as a vaporium, where pine vapour was inhaled, and a gargle room. Catering for those with breathing conditions, the 122-bedroom hotel claimed to have the 'most varied and perfect system of baths in the kingdom'. Spring water was even imported from the Auvergne in France, famous for its health-giving H_2O (Volvic mineral water comes from here). The foundation stone was laid by King Oscar II of Sweden and Norway, whose wife took an interest in the medical treatments.

Named after the French spa town that pioneered the 'Mont-Dore cure', the hotel was built by Dr Horace Dobell, one of the first four doctors in Bournemouth. Sadly, no amount of medical intervention could have helped the maharaja.

Address Bourne Avenue, BH2 6EB | **Getting there** A 5-minute walk from Bournemouth Square | **Hours** Viewable from the outside only (unless you have 'Town Hall business' to attend to) | **Tip** Hotel Mont Dore was built next door to the Royal National Sanatorium (now Brompton Court retirement complex) on Sanatorium Road. Sanatorium Road has since been renamed Bourne Avenue.

103 Tregonwell/Creeke Statue

Pulling the council's chain

Following the Black Lives Matter demonstrations in 2020, many statues the world over were removed or defaced if the subjects were deemed racist. This statue of Lewis Tregonwell (who founded Bournemouth in 1810) and Christopher Crabb Creeke (an architect and the town's first surveyor) remains intact (it was touch and go for Lord Baden-Powell on Poole Quay), but that's not to say it hasn't had its own controversy.

Creeke is sitting on a toilet, which some residents and councillors found distasteful when the Portland-stone statue was erected in 1999. The council had agreed he would sit on Bournemouth Pier, but when the sculptor Jonathan Sells discovered that Creeke was Inspector of Nuisances – or sanitation officer – he felt a loo was more fitting. And funny. Mayor Keith Rawlings, who'd commissioned the piece and paid £11,000 of his own money towards, approved of the toilet humour: 'It is a witty interpretation of my request for a statue which celebrates the life of two very important figures in the history of the town'. The council asked that the toilet face away from the road.

The other very important figure is Tregonwell, who started this seaside town by building a house near the mouth of the River Bourne: hence 'Bournemouth'. He's stood over the Town Hall (see ch. 102), which has two barrels of brandy and a boat round the back. Rumours had circulated that this renowned town-creator was also involved in illegal smuggling. Look closely and you'll see footprints by the boat and two (now weather-beaten) squirrels bounding over the barrels. For Jonathan, the squirrels – considered a nuisance by the council – represent the smugglers. In one hand, Tregonwell is holding a scroll with the names of three Bournemouth-born recipients of a Victoria Cross; in the other, he's carrying a bucket and spade. There's a lot more to this playful sculpture than first meets the eye.

Address The Bournemouth International Centre (BIC), Exeter Road, BH2 5BH | Getting
there A 7-minute walk from Bournemouth Square. The statue is directly outside the BIC. |
Tip Across the road, near the BIC Roundabout, is Royal Exeter Hotel, which now incorporates
the first house that Tregonwell began building in the area in 1810. The hotel's bar is named
1812, which was the year construction was completed and he moved into his new home.

104 Trolleybus Turntable

The wheels on the bus go round and round

What's one of your happiest childhood memories? If you lived in Christchurch between 1936 and 1969, you may answer, 'Pushing the trolleybuses around on the turntable'. Nostalgic locals recall the days – after trams and before diesel buses – when trolleybuses that ran on overhead electric cables were the town's main form of public transport, and were apparently so smooth you could do your homework on them. Once a trolleybus reached the Christchurch terminus on Church Street, there was no other way to turn it around for its return journey to Bournemouth than for the driver and conductor (and other willing volunteers – no health and safety considerations in those days!) to physically push the vehicle 180 degrees on the revolving platform.

The popularity of Bournemouth's trolleybuses was such that, in 1937, they carried 26.3 million passengers. Ten years later, this figure had risen to a whopping 42.7 million. The fleet reached its peak in 1948, with 127 vehicles in operation. The Bournemouth trolleybus system was the second largest in south England, after London. Regrettably, the system became uneconomic in the 1960s and the last day of service was 19 April, 1969.

This turntable is believed to be one of only five trolleybus turntables ever to have been made in the world. The others were in Huddersfield in West Yorkshire, London, Solingen in Germany and Guadalajara in Mexico. The Huddersfield and London turntables have been demolished, making the Christchurch turntable the last remaining one in the country. You may spot other turntables around town – in Winton, Moordown and Boscombe – but these were made for delivery trucks, not trolleybuses.

The Christchurch turntable is now a Grade II-listed 'building' and sits in the courtyard of a block of flats. As the residents go about their day, let's hope they realise how much joy this circular piece of metal once brought so many children.

Address Castle Manor Apartments, 2a Wick Lane, Christchurch BH23 1FJ | Getting there Bus 1, 1a or 1b to Christchurch Town Centre. You may have to view the turntable through the gates, if they're not open. | Tip Prior to the trolleybuses, trams were used, and Tuckton Bridge was constructed in 1905 especially to carry them across the River Stour. At the time, it was the longest bridge in the UK to use the 'Hennebique' system of reinforced concrete, and the first such bridge to carry a tramway. A toll was required to cross the bridge until 1943.

Tutton's Well

Deep and meaningful

If you had a sore eye, what would you do? Make a doctor's appointment? Pop to the pharmacy for some eye drops? Squint it out and hope it would get better all on its own? Well, if you had been around in medieval times, you might have waited for some 'healing water' (known as the Christchurch Elixir) to arrive in your town from Tutton's Well. So pure was the mineral spring water from this well that it was believed to have medicinal properties – particularly for eye complaints – and was hawked all over the country, as well as being used locally by the monks in Christchurch Priory.

To drink, the crystal-clear water was described as 'wonderfully refreshing'. Producing around 5,000 gallons of water an hour, it quenched, bathed and did the laundry for the entire village of Stanpit until about 1915, when a typhoid scare temporarily closed it. The well was ultimately capped in 1941.

The site looked very different from how it does today. In 1859, there were two raised gravel walkways to allow access to the well during high tide, as well as a drinking trough for cattle. The well itself had a traditional bucket and chain mechanism, which was replaced with a pump by 1903. The surrounding green was used by fishermen to dry their nets, plus land contraband, and formed the hub of Stanpit village for many centuries.

Following a campaign to restore the site by the Friends of Tutton's Well, it now serves as a venue for community events such as the annual Well Being Day, where locals come together to sing, dance, meditate and hang their wishes on the Wishing Tree. If you would have walked past the area on 10 July, 2004, you'd have seen a monk, a fisherman, a smuggler, a well wench, a water hawker, a leper, and Sir William Rose, who donated the site as a public water supply in 1885 – all, in fact, locals dressed up to celebrate the well's reopening ceremony. Well, well, well…

Address Stanpit, Christchurch BH23 3ND, www.tuttons-well.org.uk | Getting there Bus 1a to Purewell Cross, then a 10-minute walk | Tip To see another local well, head to Abbots Well near Frogham in the New Forest. Located on Abbotswell Road, the spring has two 'holes' – one open and one under a wooden lid, which you can lift. For centuries, this well was the main watering place for travellers to Southampton.

106 Upper Gardens Water Tower

Once upon a time…

'Rapunzel, Rapunzel, let down your hair…' If you are a handsome prince, hoping to climb this tower to meet a trapped beauty with flowing locks, you'll be disappointed to discover that at the top of this free-standing turret is merely a colony of bats. The bottom of the tower once housed garden tools and lawnmowers but, as the wooden door was a target for vandalism (and perhaps have-a-go princes trying to enter), it was bricked up in the 1980s, so now the only access is via the roof.

But this Victorian tower wasn't built as an elaborate garden shed or a roosting site for nocturnal winged creatures. Constructed in 1885, it originally provided water for an ornamental fountain in Bournemouth Upper Gardens, as well as quenching the nearby flowers and lawns. The remains of a small sluice in the Bourne Stream can still be seen, which would regulate a waterwheel that pumped water to the tank inside the tower. Both the fountain and waterwheel were removed during World War II, some of the metal being sold in the 'scrap for victory' drive to help the war effort.

Another local water tower with a similar fairytale-esque appearance is at Seafield Gardens. Built in 1898 at a cost of £2,500, it supplied drinking water to Southbourne after the pumping station at Iford went kaput. Although Seafield Gardens are less well-maintained than Bournemouth Gardens, they still contain a certain charm, and have a Fairy Garden next to the tower, complete with fairy doors, pond, bug hotel and wooden structures for kids to climb on.

Bournemouth Gardens are Grade II-listed, and split into Lower, Central and Upper. They owe much of their design to architect Decimus Burton, who also modelled London's Hyde Park, Green Park, Regent's Park, Kew Gardens, the forecourt at Buckingham Palace and London Zoo. Which, incidentally, also houses a bunch of bats.

Address Bournemouth Upper Gardens, Branksome Wood Road, BH4 9JX (note this is the address for the Gardens, not the water tower itself) | **Getting there** Park on Queens Road, walk down the slope and turn right into the gardens – a 3-minute walk to the tower. It's a 20-minute walk from Bournemouth Square through the Central and Upper Gardens. | **Tip** The Upper Gardens have a 'three-continent' theme, split into European, Asian and North American sections. The latter has many interesting tree species, including the giant redwood, Monterey pine, swamp cypress and river birch (search 'Bournemouth Tree Trail' at www.bournemouth.gov.uk to download more information and a map).

107 The Upside Gallery
Pillars of the community

It's amazing what a lick of paint can do. It's even more amazing what several cans of spray paint – and huge amounts of creativity – can do. Before September 2019, these pillars holding up the Wessex Way bridge were a harsh, Brutalist concrete. Today, they form The Upside Gallery, an outdoor mural gallery showcasing the street art of 11 talented artists from around the UK, many with a graffiti background, almost all with a cool pseudonym like Philth, Odisy, Bonzai, Squirl, Tea One or Tech Moon (see ch. 40).

Each of the 33-foot-tall paintings is as unique as the next. There's the intricate *Lily & Roses*, inspired by the Dovedale pattern from the V&A Museum. Then there's *Bottled Oxygen*, a breath-of-fresh-air piece depicting brightly coloured trees and mountains inside a giant bottle. The only untitled mural in the collection portrays a fisherman smuggler as a nod to the region's history in the smuggling trade (see ch. 93).

The enormous *Fly on the Wall* has the best seat in the house to people-watch. Its artist wanted to take a creature that's uncelebrated and find beauty within it, which he thinks is fitting to the area, seeing as there wasn't much beauty in these bare pillars, but the surrounding Bournemouth Central Gardens has beauty aplenty.

The project was funded by Arts Council England and curated by local creative agency Paintshop Studio, where Ricky Also – who painted the *On the Shoulders of Giants* wonder wall – is Creative Director. The imposing artwork in the gallery has attracted many visitors to this formerly uninviting place, including pupils on art trips, members of bike clubs, photographers, even fire dancers. Other parts of town could benefit from such creativity and, if the *History* mural here is to be believed (which displays a vertical infinity symbol spelling out a hidden message – can you see it?), history may just repeat itself, hopefully in the form of another gigantic outdoor gallery.

Address Bournemouth Central Gardens, Branksome Wood Road, BH2 6DA,
www.upsidegallery.co.uk | Getting there A 10-minute walk through the Central Gardens
from Bournemouth Square. The Upside Gallery is next to Bournemouth Gardens Tennis
Centre. | Tip Paintshop Studio has created a fair few murals in Bournemouth, including
the *North, South, East* and *West* ones at Lansdowne Bear Pit (the roundabout underpass
near Bournemouth train station).

108 Vereley Hill

Seeing red

When Chris de Burgh sang about his 'Lady in Red', it's doubtful he had a smuggler from the 19th century in mind. Dancing cheek to cheek was likely the last thing on Lovey Warne's mind as she stood on Vereley Hill in a red cloak, acting as a human beacon to warn her brothers John and Peter (as well as others smuggling tea, wine, brandy, tobacco, lace and silk) of approaching customs men. When night fell, a lantern would be hoisted to the top of the highest oak tree on this hill to signal the coast was clear. When this tree was cut down, the iron hook on which the lantern had been hung was found embedded into the top branch.

Lovey was part of the notorious Warne family, who was believed to have run the Christchurch smuggling ring in the early 1800s. Warnes Lane in Burley is named after them. John, Peter and Lovey lived in a house at Crow Hill, which was perfectly positioned for transporting contraband due to the number of tracks that converged at the house. One such track was Smugglers Road. Running through Burley, past Picket Post and ending at Ridley Wood, it's around 6.5 miles and can still be walked today. If you choose to yomp it out, you may want to reward yourself with a cold pint of Lovey Warne ale, made by Ringwood Brewery, its amber colour symbolising her scarlet cloak.

Ms Warne wasn't just a lookout girl, though – she also played an active role in sneaking goods from the ships arriving from France past the officials. She'd conceal silks and lace under her clothes and brazenly walk past customs men, safe in the knowledge that they weren't allowed to search women. This hustle came to an abrupt end, however, when one official got a little fresh with Lovey after a few drinks and began touching her thighs, getting close to the hidden silks. Lovey elbowed him in the eye and made her getaway. No way was the scarlet smuggler going to be caught red-handed.

Address Vereley Hill Car Park, Coach Hill Lane, Burley, Ringwood BH24 4HH | Getting there Note that a satnav will take you to a private residents' road. Also, be sure to park at Vereley Hill Car Park, not Vereley Car Park. | Tip The thigh-touching/eye-elbowing incident happened in the Eight Bells Inn in Christchurch, which is now a gift shop and haberdashery called Ye Olde Eight Bells Shoppe (www.twycraft.co.uk).

109 Walton House

Home of the ultimate paperman

John Lewis… Ann Summers… Max Factor (see ch. 31)… These companies have become so well established that we forget they are the names of actual people. Add to the list W. H. Smith – or William Henry Smith, to give him his full name. William was the founder of British retailer W. H. Smith & Son, and lived in Bournemouth, in Walton House, for the last few years of his life, before he died aged 73 in 1865. He designed this grand villa himself and named it after his father, Henry Walton Smith.

Now converted into hip offices, with an onsite gym and yurt in the garden, the building is owned by Richmond Group, a loan brokerage company set up by James Benamor in 1999. Benamor became one of the wealthiest young people in the UK – with an estimated net worth of £1.1 billion – and appeared on Channel 4's *Secret Millionaire*, where he donated £136,000 of his own money to those in need.

Smith displayed similar charitable tendencies and was one of the Royal National Sanatorium's most generous benefactors, as well as one of its governors. This hospital, set up in 1855, was the first to treat tuberculosis in the country, and is now Brompton Court retirement apartments, which back onto Bourne Avenue. The onsite chapel – containing a stained-glass window, stone reredos and brass plaque all commemorating W. H. Smith – still stands but has been converted into the Great Hall Residents' Lounge.

In 1863, a row of six retail units overlooking Bournemouth Square was constructed, and WHSmith set up shop in one of them. The business – which later became the first retail chain in the world – marketed itself as 'booksellers, librarians, newsagents, stationers and bookbinders'. It served tea and cake, too, in its charming tea room. More than 150 years later, trusty 'Smiths' is still in this same location but, alas, doesn't serve tea and cake any more. It probably stocks this book, though.

Address 56–58 Richmond Hill, BH2 6LT | Getting there A short walk from Bournemouth Square. Walton House has The Norfolk Royale Hotel on its left and Portman House on its right. It's inaccessible to the public via car due to a barrier on the driveway, so you'll need to get there on foot. | Tip On the front of Walton House, you'll find a blue plaque commemorating William Henry Smith. There are three more blue plaques on Richmond Hill: at The Granville Chambers, The Norfolk Royale Hotel and above the entrance to Richmond Chambers, which was the birthplace of Hubert Parry, who composed the famous hymn 'Jerusalem'.

110 West Cliff Drains

Party time

Politicians: love them or loathe them, you probably (hopefully) don't want them to get blown up. Neither did the security team who checked each of these drains for bombs, then added a blue seal stamped with a crown. Left from the last Conservative Party Conference held in Bournemouth, in 2006, they start outside the Highcliff Marriott Hotel and stretch all the way around the Bournemouth International Centre (BIC), where the conference was held. You can see the occasional red seal, from previous Labour Party Conferences, that weren't replaced with blue ones.

The Highcliff Marriott has held many smaller political conferences over the years, hosting the likes of Clement Attlee, Harold Wilson, John Major, Tony Blair, Gordon Brown and David Cameron. This hotel also holds a greater political significance; from here, the course of the history of the world was changed. In May, 1940, following a meeting at the hotel, Labour Party leader Clement Attlee phoned Downing Street from here, informing them that Labour would only join a national government if Neville Chamberlain resigned as prime minister. Within two hours, King George VI had asked Winston Churchill to step up. Attlee became the deputy prime minister, and the most important coalition government in British history was formed.

Another MP who changed history was Iron Lady Margaret Thatcher. During her 1979–1990 term as prime minister, she visited Bournemouth and Poole, riding the land train along the seafront, opening the Bill Knott building at the RNLI, partying with The Beverley Sisters at the Tory Party Ball. She also tripped over a manhole cover at Pier Approach and sprained her ankle. As one of the most divisive political leaders, those who thought she deserved her seven-minute standing ovation at the BIC felt bad that she had taken a tumble, while those who reviled her might have preferred something sinister to be lurking in the drain.

Address West Cliff, BH2 5DU | Getting there A 12-minute walk from Bournemouth Square; bus 50 to Beacon Road | Tip From political views to sea views, enjoy a meal or cocktail on the terrace of Brasserie Blanc at the Highcliff Marriott (www.brasserieblanc.com).

111__Whale Tail
Moby sick

As you sip a coffee from Prom Café under this giant whale tail, take a moment to consider Bournemouth's whale *tales*. The first began on 5 January, 1897, when a 40-tonne blue whale was struck by a ship and washed ashore. The coastguard soon claimed the 70-foot creature for the queen (a whale is a 'royal fish' and any that are beached on the shores of the UK are the property of the monarch).

Crowds gathered and schoolmasters would give lectures next to the immense animal, which had also become the source of much entertainment for children, who climbed up it and slid back down. The carcass was auctioned for £27 and most of the blubber was dumped off Brownsea Island. The rest was auctioned at the King's Arms pub at Poole Quay for the meagre sum of five shillings, despite the auctioneer trying to drum up bids by proclaiming the importance of blubber for soap and manure. The whale's skeleton was mounted on a frame and displayed on Boscombe Pier, where it remained until 1904.

Bournemouth's second 'tale from the deep' comes courtesy of a 600-gram lump of ambergris, also known as whale vomit, worth up to £40,000. The substance, which becomes smooth, compact and waxy after many years of floating in the ocean, is very rare and is used in perfumes to prolong the scent.

In 2012, eight-year-old Charlie Naysmith found this 'floating gold' on the beach at Hengistbury Head. His discovery made local, then national, then international news, with *The Ellen DeGeneres Show* even running a segment on it. The BBC's *The Treasure Hunters* bought some of the ambergris from Charlie for a few hundred pounds but, alas, a big payout never materialised. Likely due to the fact that a synthetic version of ambergris is now commonly used in the perfume industry as the real deal is associated with whaling. Still, Charlie is holding onto his sick find as a reminder of his fun five minutes of fame.

Address Pier Approach, BH2 5AA | Getting there A 10-minute walk from Bournemouth Square through the Lower Gardens | Tip Take a 20-minute walk along the promenade to Alum Chine Beach, which is where a northern bottlenose whale became beached in 2009. Locals named it Gilbert after Nick Gilbert-Smith, the RNLI lifeguard who first spotted it.

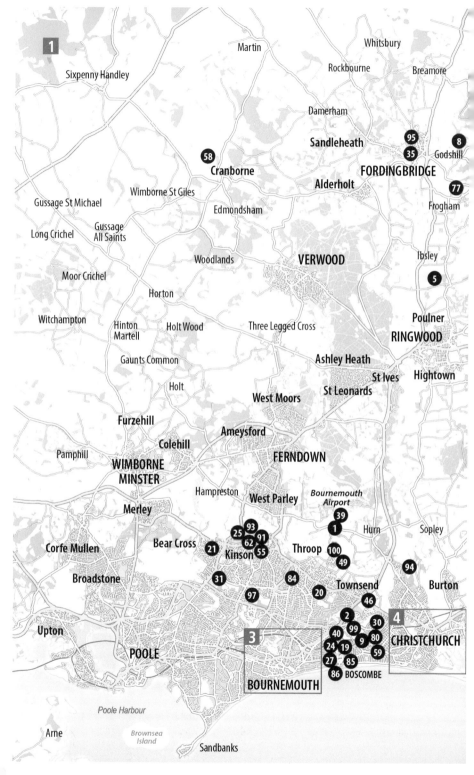

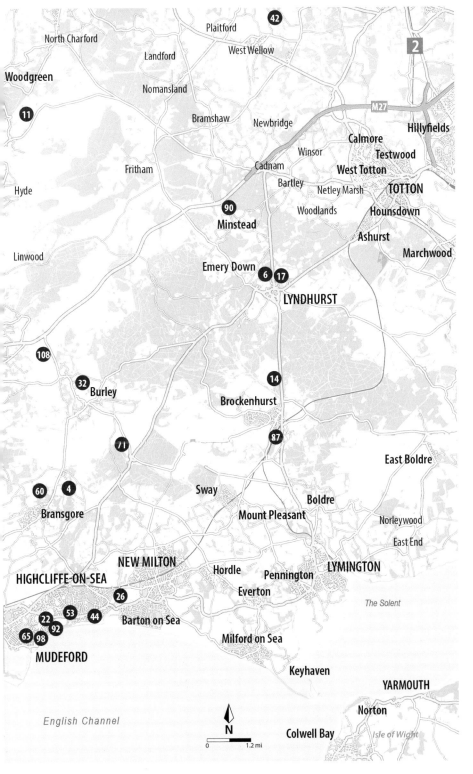

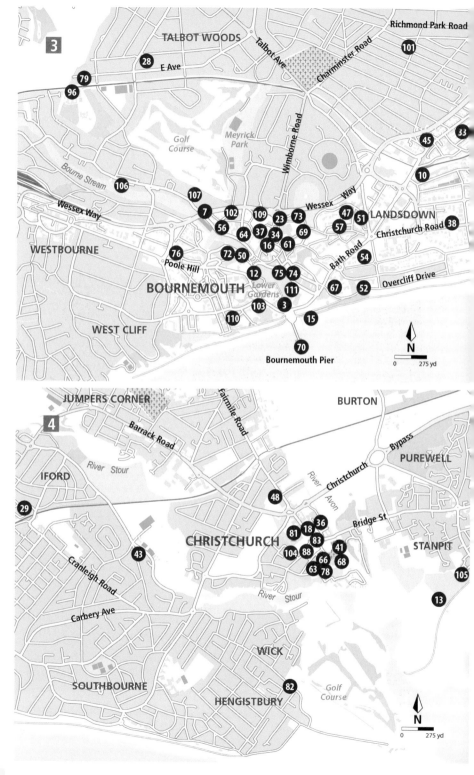

Katherine Bebo, Oliver Smith
111 Places in Poole
That You Shouldn't Miss
ISBN 978-3-7408-0598-2

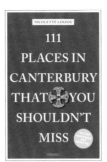

Nicolette Loizou
111 Places in Canterbury
That You Shouldn't Miss
ISBN 978-3-7408-0899-0

Ed Glinert, David Taylor
111 Places in Yorkshire
That You Shouldn't Miss
ISBN 978-3-7408-1167-9

Philip R. Stone
111 Dark Places in England
That You Shouldn't Miss
ISBN 978-3-7408-0900-3

John Sykes, Birgit Weber
111 Places in London
That You Shouldn't Miss
ISBN 978-3-7408-1168-6

Ed Glinert, Marc Zakian
111 Places in London's East End
That You Shouldn't Miss
ISBN 978-3-7408-0752-8

Solange Berchemin,
Martin Dunford, Karin Tearle
111 Places in Greenwich
That You Shouldn't Miss
ISBN 978-3-7408-1107-5

Nicola Perry, Daniel Reiter
33 Walks in London
That You Shouldn't Miss
ISBN 978-3-95451-886-9

Kirstin von Glasow
111 Gardens in London
That You Shouldn't Miss
ISBN 978-3-7408-0143-4

Laura Richards, Jamie Newson
111 London Pubs and Bars
That You Shouldn't Miss
ISBN 978-3-7408-0893-8

Emma Rose Barber, Benedict Flett
111 Churches in London
That You Shouldn't Miss
ISBN 978-3-7408-0901-0

Solange Berchemin
111 Places in the Lake District
That You Shouldn't Miss
ISBN 978-3-7408-0378-0

Rob Ganley, Ian Williams
111 Places in Coventry
That You Shouldn't Miss
ISBN 978-3-7408-1044-3

Martin Booth, Barbara Evripidou
111 Places in Bristol
That You Shouldn't Miss
ISBN 978-3-7408-1612-4

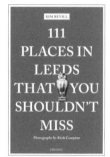

Kim Revill, Alesh Compton
111 Places in Leeds
That You Shouldn't Miss
ISBN 978-3-7408-0754-2

Julian Treuherz,
Peter de Figueiredo
111 Places in Manchester
That You Shouldn't Miss
ISBN 978-3-7408-0753-5

Julian Treuherz,
Peter de Figueiredo
111 Places in Liverpool
That You Shouldn't Miss
ISBN 978-3-7408-1607-0

Michael Glover,
Richard Anderson
111 Places in Sheffield
That You Shouldn't Miss
ISBN 978-3-7408-0022-2

Alexandra Loske
**111 Places in Brighton and
Lewes That You Shouldn't Miss**
ISBN 978-3-7408-0255-4

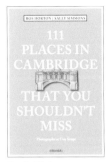

Rosalind Horton,
Sally Simmons, Guy Snape
**111 Places in Cambridge
That You Shouldn't Miss**
ISBN 978-3-7408-0147-2

Justin Postlethwaite
**111 Places in Bath
That You Shouldn't Miss**
ISBN 978-3-7408-0146-5

Gillian Tait
**111 Places in Edinburgh
That You Shouldn't Miss**
ISBN 978-3-95451-883-8

Tom Shields, Gillian Tait
**111 Places in Glasgow
That You Shouldn't Miss**
ISBN 978-3-7408-1488-5

Gillian Tait
**111 Places in Fife
That You Shouldn't Miss**
ISBN 978-3-7408-0597-5

Kai Oidtmann
**111 Places in Iceland
That You Shouldn't Miss**
ISBN 978-3-7408-0030-7

Andrea Livnat,
Angelika Baumgartner
**111 Places in Tel Aviv
That You Shouldn't Miss**
ISBN 978-3-7408-0263-9

Sybil Canac, Renée Grimaud,
Katia Thomas
**111 Places in Paris
That You Shouldn't Miss**
ISBN 978-3-7408-0159-5

Thomas Fuchs
111 Places in Amsterdam
That You Shouldn't Miss
ISBN 978-3-7408-0023-9

Rüdiger Liedtke
111 Places in Mallorca
That You Shouldn't Miss
ISBN : 978-3-7408-1049-8

Alexia Amvrazi,
Diana Farr Louis, Diane Shugart,
Yannis Varouhakis
111 Places in Athens
That You Shouldn't Miss
ISBN 978-3-7408-0377-3

Jo-Anne Elikann
111 Places in New York
That You Must Not Miss
ISBN 978-3-95451-052-8

Kim Windyka, Heather Kapplow,
Alyssa Wood
111 Places in Boston
That You Must Not Miss
ISBN 978-3-7408-1558-5

Amy Bizzarri, Susie Inverso
111 Places in Chicago
That You Must Not Miss
ISBN 978-3-7408-1030-6

Laurel Moglen, Julia Posey,
Lyudmila Zotova
111 Places in Los Angeles
That You Must Not Miss
ISBN 978-3-7408-0906-5

Floriana Petersen,
Steve Werney
111 Places in San Francisco
That You Must Not Miss
ISBN 978-3-95451-609-4

Dave Doroghy, Graeme Menzies
111 Places in Vancouver
That You Must Not Miss
ISBN 978-3-7408-0494-7

A book requiring such a vast amount of research could never be achieved without the help of others. A huge, huge thank you to local historian Mike Andrews – you were particularly generous with your time and knowledge, and without your obliging input this book would be quite different. Thanks also to Rob Bury and Hilary Forrest for taking the time to teach me all about Christchurch Priory – what a beautiful, fascinating building. Pam Field, you also deserve my gratitude – I very much appreciate you introducing me to Tahemaa, the Egyptian mummy, while the museum was closed to the public due to lockdown. A special shout-out to the members of the Memories of Old Poole & Bournemouth Facebook group; you were more helpful than you can ever imagine. Thank you to the admins for approving my many random questions.

Photographer extraordinaire Oli Smith, you've done it again! Thank you for all the beautiful images that bring my words to life, and thank you to Bec for coordinating, chasing and spreadsheeting so that Oli knew where to be and when. Ros Horton, thank you for being a brilliant editor.

Mum, Dad, Ben, Josh and Toby: thank you for being wonderful research buddies. Sorry I dragged you around so many graveyards.

Katherine Bebo is a professional freelance writer. Her career has taken her to London, Dubai and Denver, Colorado… but now she's back home in the UK, enjoying the seaside with her husband and two children. She has had a handful of books published – on topics ranging from films to fitness, cocktails to outer space – plus many features for well-known publications and websites. She also wrote *111 Places in Poole That You Shouldn't Miss.*

Oliver Smith is a commercial photographer with more than 15 years' experience shooting properties, people and places all across the South of England. Following an extensive background in art and design, he gained his BA (hons) degree in photography in 2002 and ran a photographic laboratory for two years, before going freelance as Oliver Smith Photography. He lives with his wife and two children in Poole, where together they own and run Artcetera (see ch. 9), a picture framing and art supplies shop established in 1970. He continues to work amongst the high-end interiors and architectural markets, and his images have featured in a wide range of regional magazines, as well as national newspapers.